freedom to choose

by Ernest J. Gruen

Whitaker House

PITTSBURGH and COLFAX STS., SPRINGDALE, PA 15144

© 1976 by Whitaker House
Printed in the United States of America
ISBN 0-88368-072-6
All Rights Reserved

Whitaker House
Pittsburgh and Colfax Streets
Springdale, Pennsylvania 15144

Scripture passages identified *NASB* are from *The New American Standard Bible* used by permission of The Lockman Foundation © 1971 La Habra, California; all other quotations are from the *King James Version*.

Contents

DEDICATION

To my wife, Delores, a virtuous woman, whose price is far above rubies; and to my four teenagers, Michele, Renee, Michael, and Cheryl, who are a continual reward and blessing to their father; and to the praise of the glory of God's marvelous grace!

Preface

Some of the accounts of healing and deliverance have been slightly altered to protect the precious persons involved. However, the substance of each experience has been related fully intact and is true and reliable reporting.

I express my appreciation to the body of believers in the Full Faith Church of Love who went through many of these experiences with me. Without their permitting both the secretarial help of Mrs. Pat Snead and the free time to write, this book would never have come into existence. A special word of thanks to Mrs. Michelle Hiller who did extensive editing and grammatical work in placing the spoken word into a readable manuscript form. I wish also to acknowledge Frank Terrell who played a vital and important part in the encouragement and practical undergirding of this book. A very special thanks also to Phil Freeman who did valuable editing work, and to Rosemary Cappel who helped with typing the manuscript.

This is a book of systematic principles that underlie the entire Christian walk. Its purpose is to provide a broad basis of instruction and teaching that will bring balance to the deliverance ministry.

CHAPTER

1

Forgiveness And You

What would you do if, through adverse circumstances or bad investments, you found yourself in debt to one man for ten million dollars? Could you even begin to find the money to repay him? And, if your life and the lives of your wife and children were threatened as a result, what steps could you possibly take to save your family? In your despair you might throw yourself at the mercy of your debtor, promising to somehow, someday, pay him back. Even though you both knew that it was not possible.

But suddenly, the man looked at you with tears of compassion in his eyes and spoke. Imagine hearing these words... "Be on your way, your debt is forgiven. You're free." Ten million dollars cancelled just like that! How grateful you would be! Could words express the joy that would fill your heart and change your tears to shouts of joy!!

Naturally, you would immediately cancel all the debts owed to you. What about that neighbor who borrowed twenty dollars months ago? "Twenty dollars!" you laugh. "That's nothing! Go your way, brother, you don't owe me anything. I want you to be as free as I am!"

That certainly sounds like a far-fetched story, doesn't it? Yet, it was recorded many years ago in the Gospel of Matthew, chapter 18. But I have changed the end of the story. This is how it really happened:

> 18:23. Therefore is the kingdom of heaven likened unto a certain king, which would take account of his servants.

24. And when he had begun to reckon, one was brought unto him, which owed him ten thousand talents.

25. But forasmuch as he had not to pay, his Lord commanded him to be sold, and his wife, and children, and all that he had, and payment to be made.

26. The servant therefore fell down, and worshipped him, saying, Lord, have patience with me, and I will pay thee all.

27. Then the lord of that servant was moved with compassion, and loosed him, and forgave him the debt.

28. But the same servant went out, and found one of his fellow servants, which owed him a hundred pence: and he laid hands on him, and took him by the throat, saying, Pay me that thou owest.

29. And his fellow servant fell down at his feet, and besought him, saying, Have patience with me, and I will pay thee all.

30. And he would not: but went and cast him into prison, till he should pay the debt.

31. So when his fellow servants saw what was done, they were very sorry, and came and told unto their lord all that was done.

32. Then his lord, after that he had called him, said unto him, O thou wicked servant, I forgave thee all that debt, because thou desiredst me:

33. Shouldest not thou also have had compassion on thy fellow servant, even as I had pity on thee?

34. And his lord was wroth, and delivered him to the tormentors, till he should pay all that was due unto him.

35. So likewise shall my heavenly Father do also unto you, if ye from your hearts forgive not every one his brother their trespasses.

The king who would take account of his servants represents Jesus Christ. Who is that first servant? It is you and I. Matthew 18:24 says that servant had a debt of ten thousand talents, which is ten million dollars in our money. It represents the gigantic debt we owe to God. The first part of verse 25 reads, "But forasmuch as he had not to pay..." When we look at our debt of sin—at everything wrong which we have done or thought—and at how God has put up with us and loved us and forgiven us over and over again—it is like a ten-million dollar debt that is impossible for us to repay. "Forasmuch as he had not to pay," accurately describes our condition. There is no way we can pay our debt of sin. There is no way we can deserve forgiveness. You and I deserve hell. Even if we became God's slaves, it wouldn't pay the debt.

So the Lord, according to verse 27, was moved with compassion and loosed him and forgave him the debt. That speaks of Calvary. God looked down out of heaven and He loved you and me so much that He forgave us our debts on Calvary's cross, just because He loved us.

After Jesus was nailed to the cross, the Scriptures indicate that he hung there for six hours. During the last three hours, from noon to three, the sky turned black and refused to shine. At noon He cried out, "My God, my God, why hast thou forsaken me?" He looked up and found He was cut off from God. He was separated. He was estranged. This One Who never sinned, Who had never had a dirty thought or a wrong motive, Who had never sinned in word, deed, or thought, looked up and God was gone. Can you imagine what it was like to have been in fellowship with God as Jesus was and then to look up and find God to be gone? At this point, all of our sin, rottenness, and filth, everything that we have done wrong, was laid on Jesus, and God could no longer look at His Son because of our sin. Therefore, Jesus cried out with this pathetic cry, "Eloi, Eloi, Lama Sabachthani?" ..."My God, my God, why hast thou forsaken me?" God could not look upon our sin, upon His Son, and Jesus was cut off, damned. When Jesus cried out those words, it was the most horrible cry that was ever uttered from this earth. Even the angels must have shuddered with horror at the spectacle of the Son of God hanging between heaven and earth, cut off and damned because of our sin. In fact, the Scriptures say in Galatians 3:13, "Christ has redeemed us from the curse of the law, being made a curse for us: for it is written, Cursed is every one that hangeth on a tree." Jesus was damned for our sins. Jesus was cursed that we might not be cursed. Jesus was damned that we might not be damned. He died that we might live. And this is the reason why we can be forgiven. Not because we're good. Not because we're righteous. But because Another died for our sins. He was our substitute. And because He was judged for our sins, we don't have to be judged. He loved us that much. Therefore, on the cross, Jesus Christ cancelled our $10,000,000 debt.

Now continuing with the parable, we learn that same servant went out and found one of his fellow servants who owed him one hundred pence, which is twenty dollars in our money. Do you see what Jesus is saying? The servant who had just been forgiven a ten-million dollar debt walks out the door, finds a fellow servant who owes him twenty dollars, grabs him by the throat and says, "Pay me what you owe!"

The second servant begged for mercy but "He would not: but went and cast him into the prison, till he should pay the debt." But the other servants tattled. They went to the king and said, "King, you know that servant that was just in here? The one you cancelled the ten-million dollar debt for?"

The king said, "Yes."

Then they went on and told the king, "Well, as soon as he left you, he found one of his fellow servants who owed him twenty dollars and ordered him to pay it, and when he wouldn't, he threw him into jail!"

The king said, "Is that right?" And he became angry. The Bible says the king sent for the wicked servant and said, "Oh, thou wicked servant, I forgave thee all that debt, because thou desiredst me: Shouldest not thou also have had compassion on thy fellow servant, even as I had pity on thee?" Then his lord, being wroth, delivered him to the tormentors.

After Jesus finished the story, I can imagine Him turning to Peter and looking him right in the eye saying, "*So likewise* shall my heavenly father do also unto you, if ye from your hearts forgive not every one his brother their trespasses."

What did Jesus mean when he said in verse 35, "so likewise?" So likewise what? Jesus had said the king delivered the unforgiving servant to the tormentors. Then he said so likewise shall you be delivered to the tormentors by His Father.

Our church had a baffling problem: we preached the Word, believed the healing power of Jesus, and laid hands on the sick—but the results were quite disappointing. Although a few received their healing as a result of our prayers, the majority found no freedom at all from their physical torment. Along with a concerned group of our church members, I sought the Lord with fasting and prayer for a number of months concerning this situation.

Although we had expected Jesus to guide and counsel us through Scripture explicit on healing or effective prayer, He surprised us by going directly to the issue of forgiveness. His words recorded at the end of the parable in Matthew 18 provided the major key to our dilemma:

> "And his lord was wroth, and *delivered him to the tormentors,* till he should pay all that was due unto him. So likewise shall my heavenly Father do also unto you, if ye from your hearts forgive not everyone his brother their trespasses."

Does this scripture seem entirely remote from healing to you? Step back a few verses in Matthew and let's

11

consider the Lord's teachings. Matthew 18 records Peter's words to Jesus one day, "Lord, how oft shall my brother sin against me, and I forgive him?" Peter thought he'd be generous, "till seven times?"

The Lord answered, "Peter, not until seven times, but until seventy times seven." That's 490 times. If you forgive someone 490 times you are in the habit. Jesus is not saying that after 490 times we are to stop forgiving; this is His way of saying, "Continuously."

What are the tormentors to whom God will deliver us if we do not forgive our brother from our heart? They are nerves, migraine headaches, insomnia, heart attacks, ulcers, colitis, etc. And nobody—no preacher, no faith healer, nobody—can pray the prayer of faith for us to be healed if *we* do not forgive, because it's the Father that has delivered us to the tormentors. Jesus cannot break His Word which says that unforgiveness will result in our being delivered to the tormentors.

A lady who heard our church radio broadcast called and said, "I have a goiter. Would you pray for my healing?"

I said, "All right, I'll pray for you right over the phone." I said, "You goiter, I take authority and dominion over you in the name of Jesus Christ, God's Son. I command you to loose her and let her go, now, in Jesus' name."

When I said that, a demon spoke to me. (The gift of discerning spirits includes the ability to hear or see in the spirit world.) I can still hear what he said. In an insidious, sassy tone he announced, "I don't have to let her go; she's got hate in her heart." Then I stopped rebuking and started praying in the Spirit. Immediately, the Lord said to me, "Mother and sister-in-law."

I asked, "Sister, do you have hate in your heart toward any person in your family?"

She said, "Yes, my mother and my sister-in-law," and then she named a third relative.

I continued, "Let's pray this way: (notice the Godhead) Father, in the name of Jesus, by the Holy Ghost, drop into my mind the names of those whom You see I need to forgive, those toward whom I have resentment, bitterness, or unforgiveness." I asked her then to pray for each name individually: "Father, as You forgave me when I did not deserve to be forgiven, so likewise I forgive so-and-so whether he deserves it or not, in the name of Jesus."

As she prayed, I saw a vision in my mind's eye. Perhaps, it would be more accurate to say a visualization. I saw a cylinder of bright polished chrome, as in a communion set. I looked down into it and saw the interior covered with filth. As she named the names and forgave them, it became progressively cleaner. Finally, there were two specks on the side and one speck on the bottom. I said, "Sister, you've got three more names."

She named two more names and the two specks came off the side. I said, "You've got one more and it is on the bottom of your heart."

She answered, "Yes, I know who it is. I forgive that one, too, in the name of Jesus." The last speck disappeared and the cylinder was absolutely clean.

I said, "Now I command you, spirits of resentment, bitterness, hate, and unforgiveness—and you goiter, too—in the name of Jesus Christ loose her and let her go."

She said, "I'm sick. I'm going to vomit." She set the telephone down, ran into the bathroom and vomited, and was instantly healed.

This incident illustrates one principle which the Lord showed us was involved in healing. It is quite simple—you cannot heal a demon! You can cast out a demon; but you cannot heal a demon.

My first realization of this came after preaching at a

meeting of the Full Gospel Business Men's Fellowship International in Emporia, Kansas. A man came up to me with a fungus growth. I prayed and asked the Father in the name of Jesus to heal him. As I turned around to walk away, God spoke to me, "That is a demon." I blinked. I was shocked and amazed; I could hardly believe it.

I turned around to my brother and said, "I believe that is a demon."

He said, "I know it is." That shocked me, too. I rebuked it and it came out of him. This incident was followed by no less than twelve other people being delivered instantaneously of various allergies such as sinus and asthma through deliverance. It was amazing!

That night changed my ministry. I went back to my home church in Kansas City, Kansas, and told my flock what I had discovered.

One of my daughters had had a chocolate allergy since birth. After eating only one piece of chocolate candy, or drinking half a glass of chocolate milk, her whole elbow area and wrist would break out. We would eliminate chocolate from her diet for a few months, and it would clear up except for one small spot. Then the other three children would be drinking chocolate milk, or having a candy bar, and she'd say, "Can I have some?"

"Well, honey, you can have a half of one." She would eat half of it and begin breaking out with a huge spot on her elbow and wrist area. That was the pattern.

I had prayed for her healing. My wife had prayed for her healing. We had asked the elders in the church to pray for her healing. Nothing had happened.

After the meeting in Emporia I told my home church, "Allergies are usually demons and you need to cast them out." Therefore, my daughter came forward when the invitation was given.

I said, "You chocolate allergy, in the name of Jesus

Christ I command you right now to loose her and let her go." She coughed involuntarily and the spirit came out of her! Within three days her wrist and elbow area completely cleared up.

Since that day, over five years ago, she's had only one reoccurrence, although she has eaten chocolate in all forms to her heart's desire. One morning about a year after her deliverance, she came into the kitchen and said, "Daddy, there is a little spot there again."

I said, "No, you don't, Satan. Loose her in Jesus' name." She coughed again and it cleared up within a day. Since that time there has been no reoccurrence.

We don't have to get hung up over whether an illness is a demon or a sickness—we have authority over both. We don't have to decide which it is because all you have to do is call it by name and say, "Allergy, I command you to come out of him in the name of Jesus." Then it looses the person and he is healed. Someone else can argue over what it was that disappeared.

Luke 4:38-39 states that when Jesus went to Simon's mother-in-law she was "taken with a great fever." It says Jesus "rebuked" that fever. That is what we are to do with sickness. We are to rebuke it; we are to stand against it. We are to tell it to get off God's property.

When my brother and his wife were stationed at Fort Riley, Kansas, a soldier boy crawled across the ledge of their window and came into their room while they were sleeping. My brother woke up and saw the soldier going through his pants pockets. He was scared, but he sat up in bed and shook his fist and yelled, "You get out of here!" with his foghorn type voice. The soldier was startled and jumped out the window.

That's what we've got to do to the devil. He's a trespasser. You are a temple of the Holy Ghost, if you are saved, and Satan has no right to walk on God's property.

Take authority over him and stop tolerating him. Say to Satan, "Get out of here, in the name of Jesus."

Many people have become confused by thinking that if you call it a demon, you mean the person is demonized. But, you see, man is a triune being created in the image of God—he has a body, a mind, and a spirit. You can have a demon afflicting your body even though you are walking with God in the light you have.

I believe sinusitis is an evil spirit. I can only recall seeing one person in my entire ministry who was not instantly cured of a sinus problem when it was rebuked and commanded to leave in Jesus' name. I have seen precious, Spirit-filled, loving Christians who had a sinus problem. They were not backslidden. They were not "demon-possessed" in any sense of the term. But a spirit was attacking their bodies. When it was told to go in Jesus' name it left. It had no choice but to leave.

Headaches can also be caused by demons. An interesting case clearly involving both the principle of authority over demons and the principle of forgiveness was a demon tormenting via a headache. While preaching at a camp retreat near Canada, I saw a woman in a white dress. The Lord told me, "She has migraine headaches. Pray for her healing."

I said, "Sister, you have migraine headaches."

In amazement, she confirmed, "That's right. How did you know?"

I replied, "The Lord spoke to me. Come." She came. I commanded, "Migraine headache, in the name of Jesus loose her and go into the deep."

She shook her head and said, "It's gone. Praise the Lord!" She had been agonizing for weeks with a constant headache. The next morning at breakfast she told me it was back again.

I said, "Well, then it's leaving again. Headache, I take

authority over you. In the name of Jesus loose her now." She shook her head and said it was gone. A half hour later she came to me and said the headache was back. I said, "Sister, we have been praying for the symptom, let's go for the cause."

I asked her to come with my wife and me to our cabin after lunch. She was a preacher's widow. I showed her Matthew 18, and she asked God to give her the names of those she needed to forgive. It took two and a half hours. She named two or three hundred names—most of them church members who had hurt them, disappointed them, let them down, criticized them, or spoken against them. The hurts and wounds had accumulated until they resulted in her taking pills for migraine headaches and nervousness. While she was in the process of forgiving everyone, she was instantly healed. We didn't even have to pray for her. Two times the headache was forced to depart only to return a short time later; but it was only when her heart was cleansed by forgiveness that her healing was secured.

Satan has many ways of trying to camouflage hate. We must be continually alert to prevent being deceived by such a simple trick as switching labels. A woman from Germany came to our church. She had been to every full gospel preacher in town. She had heard about me and thought perhaps I'd have a little more "faith and power" than anyone else. (That is a common ailment among full gospel people—they keep running from preacher to preacher hoping to find one who has really got the power, who will be able to pray the prayer of faith.)

She began, "I have had four nervous breakdowns."

"Let's turn to Matthew 18," I said.

After I explained the parable of the unforgiving servant, she said, in very broken English, "I don't have unforgiveness." She said the problem was her hard life, that she had been through World Wars I and II. She even attributed it to heredity.

I told her, "Sister, I've prayed with probably two thousand people all over the United States during the past five years and it is unforgiveness."

She insisted, "I don't have unforgiveness toward anybody."

What was I to do? There was no use arguing. So I said, "Sister, I'll tell you what. You love the Lord, don't you?" She said she did. I continued, "If you did happen to have unforgiveness would you be willing to forgive?"

"Why, of course," she replied.

"Let's just leave it up to the Holy Spirit," I suggested. She agreed. I had her pray after me, "Father, in the name of Jesus, if there are any people that I have resentment or bitterness or hurt feelings or hate toward, drop their names into my mind, and I will forgive them right now." I asked her if she got any names.

She said, "Na, na, just faces of people."

I said, "What do you mean?"

"I see in my mind the village in Germany where I lived and the market place is crowded with all of my acquaintances, and I hate every one of them." It took over two hours for this woman who "didn't have any unforgiveness" to name the names and forgive each one individually.

As I was counseling with another lady, she told me, "I don't have resentment toward anyone." The Holy Spirit told me, "She calls it hurt feelings."

I asked, "What about hurt feelings?"

She said, "Hundreds of people have hurt me." The devil switched labels on her to get her out from under conviction. She forgave her father, her mother, her husband, children, and right on down the line. When she was through forgiving, the power of God went through her and she was instantly healed.

God's Spirit is love and love cannot flow—God's Spirit cannot flow—when we are filled with hate. Hate is like a dam. God wants to pour out His Spirit on us and heal us and make us whole; but He can't if we've got the Spirit of God dammed up with bitterness, resentment, hate, wounds, hurts, and hard feelings stored up through the years. The average person with whom I've prayed gets from fifty to five hundred names. We've seen literally hundreds of persons stop taking tranquilizers after they had forgiven *everybody*.

If someone tells me he is nervous, I'll turn to Matthew 18 and go through the principle of forgiveness with him. It may take an hour. It may take two or three hours. But when we get through, many times we don't even pray for healing; he has the peace of God and is happy. He'll say, "I'm released."

Many cases are tragic. A woman in Missouri, who was taking thirty-two pills a day and going to several doctors called for prayer. I laid hands on her. The Lord told me, "Eight years old." I asked her what had happened to her when she was eight years old. She told me her older brother had molested her. She was in her late forties.

I asked her if she was willing to forgive him. She said he was dead. I said, "That doesn't matter. The resentment isn't."

She named his name, saying, "I forgive you in the name of Jesus. As God forgave me when I didn't deserve it, I forgive you whether you deserve it or not." She then began to cry and I physically felt the peace of God descend upon her.

I said, "Sister, do you feel that?"

She said, "Yes." She was released from tranquilizers.

An eight-year-old girl can hardly be seductive. She was the innocent party. But here was an innocent woman who had suffered forty years because the devil had implanted a root of bitterness in her when she hadn't forgiven.

I was praying with a man one day and the Lord told me, "seven years ago." I asked him what happened seven years ago. He said, "Nothing."

I said, "The Holy Spirit is not a liar. What happened seven years ago?" Again, he insisted that nothing had happened seven years ago. I said, "You tell me the truth in Jesus' name."

He shrieked, "I hate him!" as loudly as he could scream. Another man had committed adultery with his wife seven years ago. I told him he had to forgive the man.

He said, "He doesn't deserve to be forgiven."

I looked him right in the eye and said, "Neither did you."

We have been forgiven a ten-million dollar debt. God has loved us and put up with us and forgiven us over and over. So how can we do anything but forgive and love every other person?

One day while I was visiting with an acquaintance, she told me during the course of our conversation that she was taking tranquilizers. I said, "Sister, you have heard me preach on this. You know what is behind those nerves."

"Yes," she said, "and I know whom I hate. It's my father-in-law, and I'm going to keep on hating him."

I said, "Well, you will have to keep on taking your pills then." She was in an unrepentant state that day, but a few days later she prayed and forgave him. Then the nervousness left; the tranquilizers left, too.

Are you beginning to see why people aren't healed? They are delivered to the tormentors because of unforgiveness. You see, when the devil said to me that day, "I don't have to let her go," he knew his rights scripturally. *The devil knows whether he has a legal basis to attack or torment you.*

When my wife, Delores, and I begin to pray for

someone's deliverance, we'll start by addressing the particular tormentor. "Loose her and let her go, in Jesus' name." If it doesn't bring results, we exchange knowing glances and turn to Matthew 18. We know it is impossible to get a person really free who has hate in his heart. Hate is a door-keeper, the strong man. After the person understands the message of forgiveness and specifically prays, putting it into practical experience, then we command the spirits of resentment, bitterness, and unforgiveness to come out. The other things do, also.

The Nature of Your Problem

If you forgive everybody of everything from childhood to present, you will have nothing left but love in your heart.

God spoke to me one day and said, "You will never have any greater love than this: forgiving someone who doesn't deserve to be forgiven, for that is what My Son did for you on the cross." Christians are supposed to be full of the love of God, and yet we have resentments and irritations toward our closest friends. Love is forgiveness. We show the love of Jesus Christ when we pray what He prayed on the cross, "Father, forgive them; for they know not what they do."

God is love. Satan is hate. We've preached against smoking, dancing, and drinking—and I don't believe in any one of the three—but when have you heard a sermon on resentment? We major on minors, and minor on majors! The very nature of the devil is hate. The very nature of sin is hate. The very nature of your problem is hate, bitterness, resentment, envy, malice, hurt feelings, etc. If you want to be totally free and full of the Holy Spirit—if you want to be healed in your spirit and mind and body—you must kneel down and ask the Father in the name of Jesus to give you the names of those whom you need to forgive. It may take you two or three hours or even longer. But you must pray specifically for each name God gives you and choose to forgive just as you have been forgiven, whether they deserve it or not. Don't do a quicky job of praying!

Thirty days after I preached on forgiveness in one full gospel church people were saying, "God is still dealing with me about that sermon." It was a Bible-proclaiming church, yet full of bitterness. That is sad. You see, we are kidding ourselves if we say we are full of the Holy Spirit and at the same time hating our wife or our child or our mom or our neighbor. I don't care whether someone cheated you out of money, was unfaithful to you, or let you down when you depended on him; if you don't forgive him, it will cost *you*. It will cost your mental health, your physical health, and your spiritual well-being.

You may be thinking, "But that is salvation by works instead of grace." No, it isn't, because if you are really saved, you will love because you will have the nature of Christ. Now you have more light—you didn't see this before. Now you have more responsibility. Now you have some praying to do.

So you say, "Father, in the name of Jesus by the Holy Spirit, drop into my mind the names of those persons You see from childhood up that I need to forgive." One lady told me her uncle came to her mind. I asked her what her uncle had done to her. She said he tickled her; everytime she saw him he tickled her and she couldn't stand to be tickled. It was pure torture. The problem can be as insignificant as tickling—whatever it is, you must forgive that person.

Preacher Wasn't Exempt

When God showed me the truth about unforgiveness, I just knew *I* didn't have any. I am not a person to hold grudges and I felt sure that I didn't hold any resentment. But I prayed, "Father, just in case I do have, drop the names into my mind that You see I need to forgive." Eight names hit my mind so quickly that my head swam. What a shock!

The first name was that of a youth leader in one of my previous pastorates. She had been responsible for promoting dancing among the youth and had nearly split the church over it; she caused me more trouble than a barrel of monkeys. When the Holy Spirit gave me her name, I knew I had been nailed. God had me pinned right to the wall. I said, "Father, in the name of Jesus Christ I forgive_____ ," and I named her. You must name them! "Just as You forgave me, I forgive her whether she deserves it or not."

The next day, I saw her with her husband in the store, and I walked right up and greeted her and was able to visit with her. They hadn't seen me, because I was in another part of the store. What a joy to feel God's love toward her instead of corrosive resentment.

Another name I received was that of a man who cheated my mother out of half of her life savings by claiming bankruptcy.

The name of reality is love. If we have anything against anyone in our family, our neighborhood, our church, or our childhood, and we feel something between that person's spirit and our spirit, then we need to pray and get that resentment and bitterness out of us. We need to pray until we have perfect love for every person in the world. Then *when love flows,* since God is love, *the Spirit of God flows.* And when the Spirit flows, healing and deliverance come.

No Secret Revelation

All over the country, I encounter people to whom God

has spoken this same thing—people who have no relationship with me. But they do have a relationship with Jesus, and Jesus has told them the same thing He told me.

One little old lady with cancer had been prayed for many times and was not healed. She and her husband had a little cabin. She had him take her up to their cabin and leave her there. "I'm going to fast and pray for three days," she said. "Then you come and get me."

God spoke to her and said, "Get all the hate out of your heart from your childhood up." In those three days she searched her heart and forgave every single person, then was instantly healed of cancer. You see, it is hate that keeps the Spirit from flowing. Hate can keep a person from being healed.

Another example: A woman called us who had heard our radio broadcast. "Brother Ernie, they put a curse of black magic on me," she said.

"Well, that is no problem for the blood of Jesus," I replied. "You must agree with me." Then I said, "You curse of black magic, I break your power in the name of Jesus by the blood of the Lamb."

She called back a few days later and said, "It didn't work."

I said, "There is something wrong. I'm going to pray again."

She called back about three days later and said, "Brother Gruen, it didn't work."

I said, "Sister, the Bible says resist the devil and he will flee from you. There must be something wrong with your resistance." So I started praying in tongues to get discernment and then I said, "Do you really want to know what your problem is? It isn't black magic."

She said, "Oh yes, it is black magic."

I said, "No, it isn't. Do you want me to tell you the truth? It will make you mad." God had given me a word of knowledge.

She said, "No, I wouldn't get mad at a servant of the Lord." (And she didn't.)

I said, "You've got bitterness in your heart towards whole families of people. Isn't it true?"

It shocked her. She confessed, "It is true." She asked if I were going to pray for her.

I said, "I would be wasting my time unless you do something first." I told her how to pray in forgiveness. Then, I said, "When you get through naming the names, then I will come pray for you."

She called back about a week later and said, "Brother Gruen, it took me five days to get finished naming the names. I know I had more than five hundred names of people both living and dead."

If you haven't already prayed this way, you need to. If you are suffering with headaches, you can be free. If you have nervous tension, it undoubtedly is because of bitterness and resentment in your heart. That is as plain as I can make it. Don't feel like you are the only duck in the pond. The people you meet every day are in the same boat you are; that is, if they haven't already prayed and forgiven in this way.

Praying Power

Jesus said, "You can say to a mountain, be thou removed and be thou cast into the sea, and if you do not doubt in your heart, you will have whatever you say. Therefore, I say unto you, whatsoever you desire, when you pray, believe that you have received it and you shall have it." That is prayer power! But Jesus wasn't through speaking yet. He continued by saying, "And when you stand praying, forgive..." He said if you don't forgive, neither will the Father forgive you (Mark 11:23-26). Do you know why you don't have prayer power? H-A-T-E: resentment and bitterness.

When you pray, the first name you get might be your

mother or father or wife or husband or children. One of the first names I got was one of my children. I felt resentment toward the child. I didn't know why the resentment was there. I asked, "Lord, why do I resent my own child?"

He answered, "The child is too much like you." Each time I looked at this child I saw myself. Some of you reading this may have the same problem. This doesn't mean that when the Holy Spirit gives you a name, you don't also love that person. It simply means that because of your close relationship Satan has tried to cause a division between you. I love my wife with all my heart, but when she does something that irritates me, I have to forgive her for it. It isn't that I don't love her; it's just that there is a little resentment, a little bitterness or a hangup.

Maybe your wife is naggy or perhaps your husband is inconsiderate. Maybe your father wasn't affectionate. While talking with a sister I asked, "What kind of relationship did you have with your father?"

She said she didn't know him. "You mean he left home?"

"No," she replied, "he was there. He provided for us, but I didn't really know him. He never did hold me, never showed any affection and never expressed real care for me."

A man who had heard our radio broadcast called and explained that although they shared a house, he and his wife had been estranged for nearly a year. You don't need much discernment to know a marriage like that is in trouble. I visited them, opened the Bible to Matthew 18, went through it with them, then said to the husband, "You're the head of the home. Do you want to start?"

He said, "Father, in the name of Jesus drop into my mind the names of those I need to forgive." I'll never forget it. He began to cry and got choked up. Kneeling

26

there he sobbed, "Daddy, I forgive you in the name of Jesus." Then he turned to his wife, put his arms around her and said, "Honey, I forgive you in the name of Jesus." Tears of healing flooded down his cheeks as the dam of resentment burst. An hour later they were through their list of names.

A year later, the wife wrote me a letter thanking me and said, "We've had a brand new marriage ever since that Saturday morning when we forgave each other." It makes God's heart glad to see marriages saved.

The Root's Not Physical

Whatever the physical problem, the dealing must be with the spiritual cause beneath it. Tormentors, that come in through unforgiveness, are the cause.

One day God gave me a beautiful illustration concerning root causes. He said, "We preach on the surface; then we pray on the surface; consequently we get saved on the surface. Going to church is like a lawnmower job on Johnson (wild) grass. We mow it off only to have it grow back again. The wild grass must be killed at the roots."

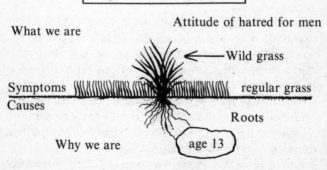

| SURFACE SALVATION |

What we are   Attitude of hatred for men

←— Wild grass

Symptoms   regular grass
Causes
                                   Roots

Why we are   age 13

So likewise we must get at the root of a person's problems. We should ask for the cleansing with the blood of Jesus, specifically, instead of the usual vague general prayers. For example, a lady came for prayer for her marriage. She was not having a satisfactory relationship with her husband. The Lord spoke to me, "Age thirteen." She had been molested by her father. With tears streaming, she chose to forgive her father. She asked the blood to cleanse her of hatred towards him; towards men in general, and towards the sex relation in marriage. She not only received a new marriage relationship, but also reported that she no longer resented her little boy. She had resented him, simply because he was a male.

We had prayed with her on the root level rather than a quicky surface prayer. Psychology can expose roots, but without the blood of Jesus there is no way to experience cleansing or healing. When the sinful attitude is repented of and cleansed by Jesus' blood, wholeness and transformation take place.

Now you can understand the absurdity of Peter's question, "Lord, how oft shall I forgive my brother, till seven times?" Forgiveness is not optional; it is an absolute imperative and is to be as limitless as God's love.

Hate Destroys

Even if I were a non-Christian, I still would not let any hatred into my heart, because of what I know. I do not want to be destroyed. Hatred destroys you. Bitterness destroys you. Resentment destroys you. It's extremely self-destructive to hate. If you resent someone, he may not even know it. He'll be happy as a lark, but you'll be eaten up, destroying yourself with headaches, nerves, and insomnia. Isn't that stupid? Nobody is more foolish than someone who lets hate ruin his life.

Did you ever hear the Lord's prayer? "Lord, forgive my

debts as I forgive..." Are you sure you want to pray the Lord's prayer? Jesus, after he said, "Amen," decided He had better underline one little phrase in the Lord's prayer so that we would be sure not to miss it. He said, "For if ye forgive men their trespasses, your heavenly Father will also forgive you. But if ye forgive not men their trespasses, neither will your Father forgive your trespasses" (Matthew 6:14-15). What you are praying in reality is, "Lord, if I do not forgive, please send me to hell!"

Wounded Spirits

Some of you have been wounded deep down in your spirit. If you have wounds, you may need someone to pray with you further, lay hands on you and ask the Holy Spirit to heal your broken heart. Jesus said, "I have come to heal the broken-hearted. I have come to set at liberty those that are bruised" (Luke 4:18). I have laid hands on people and seen the bruises and the cuts.

I was teaching at a black camp meeting once and a dear old saint about eighty years old came up to me. I laid my hands on her head and saw a vision. I saw her spirit, and it looked as if it had been chopped into a hundred pieces by an onion chopper. I said, "Lord, what does it mean?"

He said, "She has been chopped and hurt and wounded just like that in her spirit, and your race did it." I stood there and cried. God said, "You ask her for forgiveness as a representative of the white race."

I said to my sister, "This is what I see your spirit is like..." Then I asked, "As a representative of the white race, will you forgive us?"

She began to cry. She said, "I forgive you." The Holy Spirit went through her like a bolt of electricity from the top of her head to the toes of her feet, and she was made whole.

We don't know the wounds that some people have.

When you have been healed of *your* wounds, you will no longer say, "Well, I have my problems, too. What is she so upset about?" Instead you cry and say, "God, I want to pray for that man or that woman and ask the Holy Spirit to make him whole."

On one occasion, I stood in my pulpit and looked out over the congregation. As I saw the faces of my flock, God instantaneously flashed across my mind their wounds and hurts. Some of them had been through two or three marriages. I just stood there in the pulpit and wept. The needs of people! The wounds of people! The heartaches of people! They don't need someone to put them down. They need someone to love them, to get down on his knees and cry with them and pray with them. *That is what the baptism in the Holy Spirit should do for you. It should give you sensitivity and understanding, a love and an ability to minister to the needs of people.* I could not tell you in this book the hurts and wounds that I have seen. Approximately one out of every ten women I deal with has been molested by a close relative. Sometimes even by their own brother or father.

We need to quit putting people down and start understanding them. We just don't know what they've been through. If you would understand what your mom and dad have been through, you wouldn't pick at them. You wouldn't feel so bad toward them. You'd cry about it.

If God has given you ears to hear this message, you'll pray. Don't let the devil take this message out of your mind. Don't let him rob it from you, but let it change you. Reading this book will be a waste of time if you aren't, as a result, changed by it. But if you've heard what the Scriptures say, you'll obey God—and you'll be a brand new person on the inside. You'll never be the same again. I've seen these results again and again in my own life and ministry.

"How" To Forgive

Up to this point we have discussed the absolute imperative of forgiveness. Having been forgiven of so much by our wonderful Lord Jesus Christ, we see that we can do nothing else but forgive all those who've hurt us and wounded us. Since Jesus has cancelled our ten-million dollar debt, we must cancel all the twenty-dollar debts that people owe to us. We must pray saying, "I release them from any debt they owe me."

Forgiveness is not optional. It is an absolute must.

But it is senseless to even think about praying for God to give us the names of persons we need to forgive if we are going to become more emotionally upset and not deal with any of them. It is dangerous to pray that prayer if you don't understand and believe that when you choose to forgive someone in the name of Jesus, it's done—finished.

We must understand that *forgiveness is not an emotion. It is a choice.* Forgiveness is not mental gymnastics—it is not attempting to strain your mind into thinking in a new thought pattern; it is a decision that you can make in prayer.

Jesus said in John 14:14, "If ye shall ask anything in my name, I will do it." Read this verse as if the Son of God Himself were speaking directly to you, "If you ask anything in my name, *I will do it.*" Now let us suppose that you have a deep resentment for a relative. You do not have to pretend that you really do not have resentment, but quite the opposite. Go right to God, admit it and confess it for what it is. You should pray in this manner.

> Dear Lord Jesus, You know that I have deep resentment and maybe even hate for _____. I call it what it is; it is sin. I ask You to cleanse this resentment out of me with Your blood. As a definite act of my will, I choose to forgive whether he deserves it or not. You forgave me when I didn't deserve it, and so likewise I forgive him even though he doesn't deserve to be forgiven. Jesus, I ask You

31

to give me, by grace, *Your* love for him, because mine is inadequate. You promised me in Your Word if I asked anything in Your name, You would do it. I have asked You to cleanse this resentment out of me and You have. I have asked You to give me Your love for him, and so now I have Your love for him.

Then perhaps God will lead you to pray other things in reference to the person who has offended you. You might ask God to give him a tender and kind spirit instead of a harsh, critical attitude. You may ask the Lord to save him if he has not yet been born-again. You might pray earnestly for his deliverance from an evil spirit if you sense that to be his need. Parenthetically, let me remind you that the Scriptures say we wrestle not against flesh and blood, but against principalities, powers, rulers, and evil spirits (Ephesians 6:12). Therefore, it is all right to get mad as long as you get mad at the devil instead of the person. In fact, the Scriptures even command us to get angry, but not to sin. We read in Ephesians 4:26, "Be ye angry, and sin not: let not the sun go down upon your wrath." This sentence is a direct command in the original language.

After having prayed in the above manner, you will be free of bitterness toward that person and have the love of Jesus for them. *If you are not convinced of this, the problem is no longer unforgiveness but unbelief.*

I remember an experience requiring forgiveness in my own life. I was so hurt by a group of my closest Spirit-baptized brothers in a church I was pastoring that I was at the point of quitting the ministry. I said in my heart, "They can take that church and run with it. Phooey on the whole bunch of them. I don't have to put up with this. I am quitting the ministry. I don't care anymore. And I don't care that I don't care. I don't even *want* to care." But I knelt down to pray and I said, "Lord, I know that this mood I am in is not of Your Holy Spirit, and I choose for You to change me, even though I do not want to change."

My wife was also deeply hurt. She is a registered nurse and she prayed, "Lord, I believe your blood is so powerful that it can *even heal us in our inner man.* There are two kinds of wounds; one with suture marks and one without a scar. So with Your blood, heal us in our spirits so that there will not even be a scar left." God did it. He healed us in our inner man. That day of sorrow has been one of the most glorious days of my life, because through it, God worked sensitivity into my heart. Sorrow is better than laughter. Blessed are those who mourn for they will be comforted.

Let me reiterate that forgiveness is something we choose to do in prayer, it is not an emotion. In fact, one of the most important principles for a Christian to grasp is that *we can choose against our own will.* The very secret of prayer is that when we choose something in Jesus' name, then the Holy Spirit is released by God inside our inner man to change us in accordance with our request. It is marvelous news to find out that even our will can be changed. It sounds like a paradox to say that one can choose against his own will; but in reality this is the power of prayer. We are not left dependent upon our own ability or strength. *The real issue is not whether we feel like forgiving, but whether we choose to forgive;* for if we choose to be willing, God has promised to even give us the desire to change. It is written, "It is God which worketh in you both to will and to do of His good pleasure" (Philippians 2:13).

This is not only the secret of forgiveness; it is also the secret of being delivered from any attitudes or habits that are contrary to the will of God. You can be delivered from smoking, evil desires, selfishness, gluttony, jealousy, witchcraft, drunkenness, a rebellious attitude, an adulterous spirit, gossip, backbiting, unchastity, a bad temper, lying, or any other sin, because when you call on God in Jesus' name to change you—then the Holy Spirit does the work.

We also must forgive ourselves. It is a sin to not love yourself. The second of the two great commandments states, "Love your neighbor *as yourself.*" There is a proper self-love. Obviously, it is different than selfishness. It is a self-love that involves self-respect. The Scriptures say in Hebrews 10:17, "Your sins and iniquities will I remember no more." If you knelt down to *reconfess* some particular, grievous sin, God would say to you, "What are you talking about?"

You might reply, "God, don't you remember?"

And God would say, "Frankly, no. I have forgotten it, now you forget it also, my child." If the Judge of heaven and earth declares you forgiven, it is the height of presumption and pride for you to not forgive yourself. It would be like elevating yourself above God. Therefore you should simply pray a prayer like this:

> Dear Jesus, You have forgiven me and forgotten my sin. I am not higher than You. Therefore, I choose likewise to forgive myself and to forget my sin. With Your blood wash away all my guilt and shame and even the remembrance of my sin, in Jesus' name. Amen.

One other aspect of forgiveness which we need to consider is our attitude toward God Himself. Many people, through sorrows and pains, trials and tribulations, become bitter toward God. Now it is obvious that God is holy and cannot sin. Consequently, He has not sinned against us, nor failed us. Therefore the problem is not our forgiving God, but rather repenting of our attitude toward God. We must *know* that it is literally true that "all things work together for good to them that love God, and to them who are the called according to His purpose" (Romans 8:28). This verse does not state that everything *is* good. There are many circumstances and trials that are evil and not good. But this verse states that God causes all things to work together *for* good. It is not *what* happens to us in life that is important, but our *response* to what happens to us in life. The same experience can make one person bitter and disillusioned, while making another person sensitive and full of compassion for others. Bitterness is a wrong response toward God. Notice also, that He causes all things to work together *for His purpose*. His purpose, according to the next verse, is that we should be "conformed to the image of His Son." The purpose of God is always fuller and richer than our temporal and carnal purposes. He causes everything to work together for *His* purpose, not *ours*.

Therefore we can pray like this:

> God, I know that You are holy and cannot sin. You do all things well. My attitude toward You has been one of questioning and bitterness. This is sin. I repent of it. Wash it out of me with Your blood. I realize that all evil comes from Satan, not from You, and forgive me for blaming You for any of the works of the enemy. I can, and I do trust You. I know that all things do work together for my good. And Father, I love You. In Jesus' name. Amen.

Before reading the next chapter, deal with this one. Stop reading and pray. Ask God to give you the names of those whom He sees you need to forgive. They will be brought into your remembrance. Forgive each one, separately. Take time to pray deeply, even if it takes you several days. In fact, names and faces (whose names you have forgotten) may continue to come to you in the following weeks.

This chapter is absolutely worthless, unless you do it!

CHAPTER

2

The Always Present Bucket?

A man called Legion: Undoubtedly one of the most demonized men in history, equal to any psychotic maniac today, or at any time in the history of the world; a man set free by Jesus. Matthew 8, Mark 5, and Luke 8, all record the dramatic encounter between Jesus and this fierce, untamable creature, who acted more like a beast than a man, and who lived among the tombs. His deliverance was quick, simple, and complete. We would do well to study these scriptures to determine (1) The characteristics of demons, and more importantly, (2) The method of deliverance in Jesus Christ.

Mark 5:1—And they came over unto the other side of the sea, into the country of the Gadarenes.

2—And when he was come out of the ship, immediately there met him out of the tombs a man with an unclean spirit,

3—Who had his dwelling among the tombs; and no man could bind him, no, not with chains:

4—Because that he had been often bound with fetters and chains, and the chains had been plucked asunder by him, and the fetters broken in pieces: neither could any man tame him.

5—And always, night and day, he was in the mountains, and in the tombs, crying, and cutting himself with stones.

6—But when he saw Jesus afar off, he ran and worshipped him,

7—And cried with a loud voice, and said, What have I to

do with thee, Jesus, thou Son of the most high God? I adjure thee by God, that thou torment me not.

8—For he said unto him, Come out of the man, thou unclean spirit.

9—And he asked him, What is thy name? And he answered, saying, My name is Legion: for we are many.

10—And he besought him much that he would not send them away out of the country.

11—Now there was there nigh unto the mountains a great herd of swine feeding.

12—And all the devils besought him, saying, Send us into the swine, that we may enter into them.

13—And forthwith Jesus gave them leave. And the unclean spirits went out, and entered into the swine: and the herd ran violently down a steep place into the sea, (they were about two thousand) and were choked in the sea.

14—And they that fed the swine fled, and told it in the city, and in the country. And they went out to see what it was that was done.

15—And they come to Jesus, and see him that was possessed with the devil, and had the legion, sitting, and clothed, and in his right mind: and they were afraid.

16—And they that saw it told them how it befell to him that was possessed with the devil, and also concerning the swine.

17—And they began to pray him to depart out of their coasts.

18—And when he was come into the ship, he that had been possessed with the devil prayed him that he might be with him.

19—Howbeit Jesus suffered him not, but saith unto him, Go home to thy friends, and tell them how great things the Lord hath done for thee, and hath had compassion on thee.

20—And he departed, and began to publish in Decapolis how great things Jesus had done for him: and all men did marvel.

Notice in verse one of Mark 5, "They came over unto the other side of the sea, into the country of the Gadarenes. And when Jesus was come out of the ship, immediately there met him out of the tombs a man with an unclean spirit." A demonized person will challenge your authority immediately. I remember teaching in a Bible class for a solid hour against "religious spirits" and "spirits of interruption." A dear lady amened every word in supposed agreement. I finished by stating that if someone has the brashness and audacity to interrupt a service the person in charge should have the same boldness to correct it. The devil didn't wait long to challenge that teaching. During the opening prayer of the service that followed, the same dear lady with the vocal amens, suddenly began to make violent gestures and loud articulate noises interrupting the prayer. It was as if the demon said, "I challenge you to back up what you just taught—I dare you to do it." So I did. I immediately called the dear lady "out of order." It was a spirit of witchcraft and domination.

The Scriptures state that this man had an unclean spirit, and dwelt among the tombs. It is interesting to note that he would choose to live with the dead, in a dead place. It is indicative of his spiritually dead condition. One may generalize concerning people who are under satanic attack: they are almost always tempted to withdraw, to be anti-social, to get off by themselves, to be a loner. They say, "Oh, I wish I could just get away from it all. If I could only escape and be alone. If I could just get away for a while." There's something about a demon that causes people to withdraw from fellowship, from the church, from society, from their husband, or wife, or children, or from life's responsibilities. *Withdrawal is nearly always manifested:* getting away, getting cut off, getting alone.

Now I suppose all of us have thoughts like that. Some

of us have fleeting thoughts; others, patterns of thoughts. But nevertheless, one of the most prominent characteristics of the demonized Gadarene was that he had withdrawn to live all by himself, alone in the cemetery. If you're thinking of withdrawing or just getting away, cutting off from God's people, cutting off from your relatives—that is an activity of demons trying to bring about an anti-social withdrawal, trying to draw you away from the fellowship that you really need.

Luke further records that the man with an unclean spirit lived naked and unclothed in that graveyard. "And when he went forth to land, there met him out of the city a certain man, which had devils long time, and ware no clothes, neither abode in any house, but in the tombs" (Luke 8:27). And after Jesus set him free, he was sitting clothed in his right mind. It is a satanic attack to disrobe and expose one's body; that is true of both men and women. The exposure of the body is a mark of demon activity. And we're living in an age where few people are controlled by Jesus Christ, and many, many people are controlled by unclean spirits. Even if they haven't fallen into adultery, they want to be seductive, and take pleasure in having others lust after them with adulterous eyes. *It is of the devil.*

A third characteristic is mentioned in Mark 5:3, "He had his dwelling among the tombs, and no man could bind him, no, not with chains." Matthew 8:28 concurs, "The two possessed with devils came out of the tomb, exceedingly fierce, so that no man could pass by that way." This man was violent; no one could tame him. He was put in chains, and he snapped the chains in two. He was the type of man whom we would put into a straitjacket today, and he would rip it to pieces with superhuman strength. "Exceedingly fierce"—that's another mark often found in demonic activity: violence, cruelty, someone untamed and out of control. In fact, the Bible tells us no one walked on that road, which went by the graveyard. They evidently avoided the entire vicinity.

Self-control, one of the fruits of the Spirit, is a virtue the devil hates. His methods for attacking it are varied, two of the most successful and common today being drugs and alcohol. It is extremely dangerous to take anything into one's body which causes loss of control. When one has lost the ability to make his own decisions, to control his own actions, he has surrendered his sovereignty to a demon spirit. A mature person remains in control of himself. He controls his appetites, his temper, his desire for possessions, food, and sexual fulfillment. Self-control is tremendously important, but the man who dwelt among the tombs had been robbed by Satan of any vestige of it.

Notice that the Scriptures relate, "Neither could any man tame him." In other words, no "psychiatrist" could help him; no "preacher" could help him; he was beyond man's help. There are people who become so trapped by sin and habits that they are beyond human help. The *only* One who can help them is Jesus Christ. The only One who can set them free is the Lord. This man was so totally out of control that his only means of release was through Jesus.

Mark 5:5 continues, "Always night and day he was in the mountains and in the tombs crying and cutting himself with stones." He was suicidal. He wanted to end his tormented life. There are many people who torture themselves in various ways trying to win atonement, trying to win favor with God, because they don't believe the blood of Jesus has cleansed their sin. This pathetic, suicidal man spent his life sobbing and torturing himself because he didn't know about the atonement.

Yet notice that, "When he saw Jesus afar off, he ran

and worshipped him." Imagine the scene as it must have appeared: a naked, filthy, beast-like man, covered with bruises and blood-caked wounds, tears streaming from his frenzied eyes, coming out of that graveyard. Surely those with Jesus must have fled in fear to hide behind the nearest tree, or rock, but our Lord received him as he cast himself at His feet in worship. What a tremendous picture!

Let us examine the basic principle involved here: *God will never allow a person's will to be taken from him.* Here is a man who seems utterly and totally controlled by the devil: violent, fierce, naked, unclean, suicidal, anti-social—yet when he sees Jesus his free will is still intact. It is false teaching to state that a man is so demonized that he cannot respond to God. It is false teaching to say, "The devil made me do it." If this demonized man, in his extreme condition, still had his free will, don't ever say, "My free will is gone." It is not! God will not permit your power to choose to be taken from you.

The first step in deliverance is to fall at the feet of Jesus and to worship Him. Regardless of who you are, or what you've done, you have a free will. The responsibility, therefore, is yours, and yours alone. If you choose to fall at His feet and worship Him, Jesus Christ will set you free.

Now, let us scrutinize the scriptural method of deliverance. Mark 5:7 tells that the demoniac cried with a loud voice saying, "What have I to do with thee Jesus, thou Son of the Most High God?" (That is the demon speaking out of him.) "I adjure by God that thou torment me not." Unfortunately, deliverance by many preachers today is not torment to the demon, but to the person going through it!

Recently, I was confronted with the horrible, confused account of a certain woman's deliverance. If I had to get rid of a demon the way that woman got rid of a demon, I would pray to Jesus and say, "Lord, couldn't you just bind it good and solid and put a gag in its mouth and leave it in there?" She went through a two-year cycle of running to and fro among preachers.

One preacher based his deliverance on a New Testament scripture where a spirit threw a person to the ground. He had the woman sit on the edge of the chair and, sure enough, what do you think the devil did? He obliged. He threw her on the floor, and she went bouncing across the room and ended up on a stack of overshoes. The evil spirit then proceeded to play "peek-a-boo" with her, entering and leaving and reentering until she was physically exhausted and spiritually and emotionally numb.

After many detailed conversations with the demons who were giving their names and much more the woman finally said, "So I had with me my *always-present bucket.*" At that point I had become totally aware of the error and horror of this method of deliverance—it was sheer torment for the woman involved.

The woman claimed she had a legion of demons, like the man in the Scriptures, but the account of her deliverance was the exact antithesis of this man called Legion. This dear sister was sincere, as were those whom God used to aid her deliverance, and yet the contrast was unmistakable.

The man called Legion was as demonized as you could ask for: a Roman legion had 6,000 soldiers in it. When those demons came out, 2,000 pigs ran down over the cliff and drowned. This man evidently had between 2,000 and 6,000 demons—only God knows. But when Jesus cast out those demons, He said one word, "Go," and they left! You don't read that he vomited, burped, coughed, gagged, choked, or got a bucket; they just left him and that was that.

Parenthetically, there was a similar problem in another area of the Spirit-filled life. At the earliest part of this century when people were first led into the baptism in the Holy Spirit, they were led into it without teaching. They did receive the baptism, but the ministry used to bring them into this experience was very inferior because of the lack of teaching. One person would yell, "Let loose, brother," while in the opposite ear another would yell, "Hang on, brother." Meanwhile, another would be spraying them with saliva, praying right in front of their face, while someone else slapped them on the back. On some occasions they received the baptism in the Holy Spirit, *despite* those working with them. Yet many did receive the baptism, and it was always when they finally believed.

The same set of circumstances is true about deliverance. A decade ago, when it was restored to the body of Christ, people received deliverance and it was real, but they received it with poor teaching and wrong methods. Workers would encourage demons to speak, which is exactly the opposite of what the New Testament teaches. The ministers would get buckets and paper towels and very foolishly command the demons to expose themselves. Satan would oblige them with amazing demonstrations.

But now the Body of Christ is learning that if we sit down and teach someone for thirty minutes concerning deliverance and then pray a simple prayer of faith and stand on a Word of Scripture, they can be set free just as easily and as simply as they receive the baptism in the Holy Spirit. They receive their deliverance on the basis of faith in the Word. Sometimes there are still manifestations, but their faith is not in the manifestation, but rather in the Word of God. People will still receive deliverance by the use of wrong methods, even as people still receive the baptism by the use of wrong methods. But now, the Body of Christ is coming into maturity in the realm of deliverance even as it has in other areas.

There are three main factors involved in deliverance. The first and most important is to get a clear discernment from the Holy Spirit as to what spirit needs to be rebuked. *The key to deliverance is discernment.* This means that we need to be in the Spirit and take the time to sit down and fellowship with the person to discover where he really is in his walk with the Lord. Once the deliverance minister receives a word of knowledge or discernment of a spirit, then that demon will have to leave when it is rebuked. Jesus never had ongoing conversations with demons. People who talk to demons are bordering on practicing spiritualism, because they are consulting demons for advice. They also reveal that they have not heard from the Holy Spirit by the gift of discerning of spirits. Therefore, the only avenue left for them to take is the unscriptural approach of talking to demons. It is true that Jesus asked the demoniac what the name of the demon was. On certain occasions we might command the demon to give us its name, but anything more than this is against the many scriptures where Jesus commanded the spirits to hold their peace. This phrase "hold your peace" in the Greek literally reads "be muzzled!"

The next two factors involved in deliverance are repentance and faith. If the tormented individual will fall at the feet of Jesus in true repentance, all that is needed to effectively accomplish deliverance is to speak in faith four words, "Go, in Jesus' name." It need not take two hours, five hours, or half the night, or three months. If we believe it will take six hours, it will. If we believe it must be accompanied by coughing, burping, gagging, choking, and an "always-present bucket," it will. If we believe demons can go in and out, they will. Satan is only too happy to oblige any negative faith in him.

One Saturday, a car drove into our driveway, and a pitiful young man emerged trembling, trying to speak through a shaky, stuttering voice. With much difficulty he finally expressed, "The devil is confusing me, he's overcome me, I don't know what I am going to do." He hadn't had any water in five days, the devil had told him it was a sin to eat, a sin to drink, he was going to have to fast and he couldn't so much as drink water if he wanted to be free. The devil told him he couldn't have a normal relationship with his wife because that would be a sin.

I said, "Brother, why don't you just sit down here on the lawn and let's talk a little bit. The devil is playing ring-around-the-rosy with you." And I began to talk to him and share with him.

He looked up in amazement, "You mean the devil is just telling me all this?"

I said, "He is dropping these thoughts into your mind. The trouble is you believe too much in the devil. You're talking to him, you're believing in him. You must get hold of yourself."

He said, "You mean I can get a drink?"

I said, "Sure." We walked over to the church, got a drink, and I talked to him about an hour and I never did rebuke any demons. But when he left do you know what he said?

"You know what, I'm going to go on a picnic with my family." The devil wanted me to spend five hours burping him! It's the truth! The devil wanted me worn out, tired, out of the Spirit, and so drained that I couldn't even preach on Sunday.

I am tired of playing "ring-around-the-rosy" with the devil. When someone comes to me, I tell him to repent, and simply command the demons to go, all of them, in

Jesus' name. If they don't leave, it is because that person didn't want them out and didn't repent and worship at Jesus' feet.

For a long time I was puzzled by the fact that deliverance for some was easier than for others. Finally, I realized that for those who are not truly repentant, deliverance will be difficult; they will fight the Holy Spirit.

Frank McLaughlin, who was our associate pastor, and I were trying to free a young woman of a spirit of adultery. She screamed at the top of her lungs for about five minutes and we couldn't budge it. Finally I said, "Stop it; I want you to talk with us privately."

After she had calmed a bit I asked, "Have you ever asked Jesus Christ to cleanse you of this adultery with His blood?"

She said, "No, I haven't."

"Now," I said, "I want you to confess every single time you committed adultery. I'm not interested in terms of curiosity and I don't mean to embarrass you, but I want you to name the first name of everyone with whom you committed adultery and specifically, one by one, ask the blood of Jesus to cleanse you."

She had lived in a commune full of immorality and wickedness and must have been in adultery fifteen or twenty times.

When she finished confessing that, I said, "You spirit of adultery, leave her." She coughed, gagged once or twice, and it was simply gone.

I learned something. If a person renounces something, really repents, and asks the blood to cleanse it out of him, that spirit is going to leave. The only reason it has trouble coming out of some people is that they still want it and haven't repented and asked the blood to cleanse it out of them.

Satan's desire and deceptive plan for the modern believing church with regard to deliverance is becoming increasingly clear. He would like us to become so side-tracked by the manifestations of deliverance that it becomes a torment in itself and we lose sight of the effective simplicity of the scriptural method. Jesus said, "You'll do greater works than I." I believe it. He said, "If you believe in me, the works that I do you shall do, and greater works." If you have a spirit, you can get rid of it with four words, "Go, in Jesus' name." If you say, "I don't believe that," that's what your problem is. You can tell that spirit of unbelief to go, also.

I believe in deliverance: I know that there are demons, but more importantly I know Jesus. If you fall at His feet and worship Him and command the demons to go, they have to go. Do not put faith in manifestations. And do not put faith in the one praying for you. Your faith must be in Jesus Christ.

I have prayed with many people this way; I have put the principles of this chapter through a crucible. One sister was so distraught I had to bind the spirits to keep her from fainting. She had been in the occult and she had been so "freaked out" she could hardly speak. I said, "I want to show you some Words." But she wanted to talk about the devil. I said, "I want to show you a scripture." And she said, "I want to tell you how bad the devil is." All she wanted to do was talk about the devil. I said, "Let me show you this scripture." And finally, after about twenty minutes, I got her to read I John 1:9.

She asked the blood to cleanse her. She overcame the demon by the blood of the Lamb. She quit praying, and said, "I'm at perfect peace now." Praise the Lord! That was pretty simple.

Well, if Jesus rid the demoniac of his horrible condition with one word, you ought to sit up and listen.

"Well," you say, "they get sick." Sometimes they do, but that is not what my faith is in. "Well," you say, "what if they burp?" Sometimes they will. But my faith isn't in whether they gag, or choke. I've seen them come out of people in all those ways, and they may *still* come out of people in all those ways. But I don't look at the manifestation, I look at Him who is the Deliverer. I'll do the rebuking, and the devil will do the leaving, regardless of the manifestation.

We rebuked a spirit one morning in our church. A sister was healed, and then she began to wail and make weird noises. I said, "Sister, that emotionalism isn't the Holy Ghost."

She said, "What did you say?"

I said, "Have you ever been to a fortuneteller?"

"Yes, sixteen years ago."

"Well," I said, "you must renounce it."

"But, it was sixteen years ago!"

I said, "I don't care, that's a religious spirit that's making you carry on like that, and it comes from your having gone to a fortuneteller."

I had the right discernment, so step two was to renounce it and repent of it. I said, "Loose her in Jesus' name." Suddenly she became dizzy. Then I said, "You have got to go!" and that demon left immediately. It was a physical manifestation of that spirit and it left.

It doesn't matter whether there are manifestations or not. Many times there will be, but *you must not put your faith in a manifestation,* or in the person praying, instead of believing in Jesus. Do you understand that? Hallelujah! Always present bucket?? Thanks to the power and authority of Jesus' name, that bucket has lost its importance.

Let us return to the account of the demoniac in Mark 5 and examine some results of deliverance. Verse 15 tells us three immediate results: he was sitting, clothed, and in his right mind. I have already discussed that one result of deliverance is that you put on some clothes. I believe that; I'm not just saying it to be humorous. I believe that a person who is right with God dresses chastely.

The second thing we notice about the former demoniac is that he is sitting. How amazed the local townspeople were to find him sitting at the feet of Jesus. It is a wonderful thing to be able to sit down in a chair and be at peace. There are people who actually can't sit down. They are nervous, fretful, always pacing back and forth; they can't relax. "Oh," they say, "just to be able to sit and relax." Something is wrong when a person can't sit. I suppose the devil would like to make us feel guilty about enjoying some peaceful time just relaxing, but it is a tremendous blessing when you don't feel compelled to pace. I know people who say, "I've got to go somewhere!" It is impossible for them to just sit. They always have to be doing something. If we have freedom in Jesus, our greatest joy is sitting quietly at His feet, clothed, and in our right mind. Hallelujah!

"In his right mind" that scripture states. I have noticed many religious people who are not in their right mind. They have all sorts of notions concerning what they're going to do for God. A man came to me and announced, "Bless God, I know I'm going to be a pastor." Every child he had was rebellious, out of order, and completely contrary to the life of Christ.

I said, "You're right, brother, God has called you to be a pastor, and your flock is your children." The Bible says if you don't have your house in order you can't be a pastor. Someone is always trying to become big in the church when he doesn't even have his own family straightened out. This is what I mean about being in your right mind. I suppose there are more religious "freaks" around than any other kind. I wish it weren't the truth, but it is. If you sat in my office and listened to people who come for counseling, you would both laugh and cry at the same time. Religious people need right minds too.

I believe God will give you a right mind. Being spiritual is not being spectacular. Most of the time, it's just simply becoming a good husband or a good wife, a good mother or a good father and a decent provider—a person who can live up to his responsibilities. That's what it means to have a right mind. It means to be able to keep a job, to get up out of bed and go to work consistently.

Most people look for temple-jumping things. The devil came to Jesus and said, "If You're the Son of God, why don't You climb up on the temple and jump, and everyone will know You're the Messiah."

Jesus said, "Thou shalt not tempt the Lord thy God."

To Christian after Christian, as soon as they are filled with the Holy Spirit, the devil comes and tells them to do some flashy, silly, or super-miraculous feat. Temple-jumping things. When you are free, you become settled, and you get your feet on the ground. You have some horse-sense and you start thinking about taking care of your wife and children. If you want to know whether you have a right mind, ask your wife or your husband.

The man, who minutes before had been wild, raging, possessed of the devil, was now sitting, clothed, and in his right mind: a complete transformation had taken place. Then we read that he petitioned Jesus that he might be with Him. That is the fourth result of deliverance. He wanted to spend time with Jesus. When someone is really free, he wants to be with Jesus.

But Jesus said, "Go to thy friends and tell them how great things..." You see, Jesus wasn't allowed to preach there anymore, so he had to leave this man behind to tell the story. "Go home to thy friends and tell them..." The fifth result of deliverance is witnessing, testifying that the Lord had compassion for you and telling the great things He has done for you.

"He departed and began to publish in Decapolis (which means ten cities) what great things Jesus had done for him and men did marvel." He obeyed; he was submissive to the Lord, and he became an evangelist to ten cities. This formerly demonized man became an obedient evangelist and was a successful proclaimer in his own immediate community.

Obviously, many people need deliverance. We have determined that one's free will is always intact, and we concluded that our method was wrong—that people have been trusting in the manifestations, rather than in Jesus. Far from denying deliverance, we have urged simply, "Let's go back to Biblical methods." Also, we've emphasized the fact that the individual in trouble is the one who must decide whether he wants to be free. There are few who are in as much trouble as this man was and Jesus set him free instantaneously. Hallelujah!

I don't think it makes a lot of difference whether the evil spirit is in you, around you, or on you. The point is that in Jesus' name it has to leave. Satan doesn't care so much where he is geographically or physically, what he cares about is how much control he exerts over your body and your personality. An interesting verse of Scripture is Mark 1:23 concerning a man in the synagogue who had a demon. Although the King James version doesn't express it this way, the original Greek of that passage is, "He was *in* an evil spirit." That's an amazing thing, to be in an evil spirit. In other words, it was a cloud covering him. Now, many of you have been in the Holy Spirit. Also some of you have been in an evil spirit; we all have at times. Just think of it like a cloud: a cloud of depression, a cloud of self-pity, a cloud of despair. It is a very strange thing to me that Jesus rebuked the spirit in which the man was and it came out of him. How can he be "in a spirit," and yet the "spirit be in him?" Well, you could try to figure it out, but I believe that the devil would love to have us argue about whether it is in, on, or around—I know this much, if there's a demon hanging around me, I know what I'm going to do. I'm going to tell it to go and I'll let somebody else worry about whether it was in or around or attached. At the name of Jesus it's got to go, and that's the point! It doesn't take ten minutes. The time involved is how long it takes us to decide that we want to repent and rebuke it. "At the name of Jesus every knee should bow, of things in heaven, and things in earth, and *things under the earth*" (Philippians 2:10). Amen!

CHAPTER

3

Avoiding The Backlash

Perhaps the easiest part of the deliverance ministry is exorcism, or the casting out of demons. As I was casting demons out of a lady one day in our church, the Lord spoke to me, "The Lord's rest even enters into the realm of deliverance." Praise God!

When we shout and scream and yell it can be unbelief. We should simply rest in the power of the Lord. The devil has to bow. "Wherefore God has highly exalted him and given him a name which is above every name: that at the name of Jesus every knee should bow, of things in heaven, and things in earth, and things under the earth." Satan doesn't have a chance. You give him orders to leave, and he has to go. *Not because of who you are, but because of who He (Jesus) is.* Jesus has a name that is higher than any other name. It is higher than Lucifer or Gabriel, or any earthly potentate. It is higher than anyone in this world, the Bible says, or in the world to come. So when you say, "Depression, in the name of *Jesus* let me go," that filthy, foul, tormenting spirit has got to get up, loose your mind, move out, and let you go.

When God said, "The Lord's rest even enters into the realm of deliverance," I went over to the prayer bench, sat down, and I literally twiddled my thumbs. I just started rebuking things—hallelujah!—and they started leaving.

A few weeks later, we were in a garage having a mass deliverance meeting. There happened to be an exercise bicycle there, so I sat down on it. As I was pumping away and rebuking demons, I thought, "Man, this is easy." I don't mean that presumptuously in any way, but the point is that *Jesus is the deliverer.* There is no one who can deliver you but Jesus. *Jesus alone* is the deliverer. Many people make hard work out of deliverance when all we need to do is rest in the Deliverer.

There is a great need for teaching in the Body concerning deliverance and how to keep it. After I was casting a spirit out of a lady one day she replied, "Well, I don't feel any different."

I explained, "I don't care if you feel any different or not, if you rebuke it and command it to go, it's got to go.

"You mean it has to go?" she questioned.

I said, "That's right."

"All right," she said, then she belched and burped. And it left her.

I refused to doubt. And because I continued to believe, that spirit had to leave.

The weakest Christian can run the biggest demon, because it isn't you, it's Jesus. You may be a little David; but I tell you there is more power in Jesus' name than there was in David's slingshot. You can kill the giant if you will rise up and see who you are in Him; or in other words, who He is in you. Just say, "In the mighty name of Jesus, go."

The devil has made us think it's hard, but it's easy. The devil likes nothing more than a seven-hour deliverance meeting that lasts until four in the morning. He loves that. But you don't find it that way in the New Testament. Jesus said one word when he delivered the man whose name was Legion. He cast out those spirits with one word. When they begged to go into the hogs, Jesus simply said, "Go!" and they went. One word "Go!" Now we have to say four words because we're not Jesus, and they are, "Go, in

Jesus' name." Hallelujah! There wasn't any seven-hour deliverance meeting. Legion's demons ran into those hogs.

An interesting phenomenon is recorded in the verse of Scripture following. You would have expected the townspeople to come and say, "Oh, hallelujah, that nut who lived out in the cemetery, and cut himself, and was naked, whom we all feared, and who broke every straitjacket we put him in—he's sane and he's clothed, in his right mind at the feet of Jesus." But they didn't say that. They said in effect, "Jesus, depart from our coast—get out of here, we don't like this monkey business of deliverance."

The deliverance ministry is never popular. When you cast out demons, people don't like it; they are afraid of you. Just as in the Bible days, someone says, "I don't believe in this demon business." You better check and find out why, because they should rejoice when a person is freed from demons.

When I was in Holland, I discovered a universal principle. The people in Holland know that Americans have demons, but Hollanders don't. And Americans think, "Oh those Africans, those pagans, they have demons." The Frenchmen know that Germans have demons. Do you see it? "Oh, sure we believe in demons—in Africa." Nonsense! They're in your church, that's where they are!

Now, in Luke 10:17, "The seventy returned again with joy saying, 'Lord, even the devils are subject unto us through thy name.'" They understood. Through what? Through the name of Jesus. "And he (Jesus) said unto them, I beheld Satan as lightning fall from heaven." Verse nineteen: "Behold, I give unto you power . . ." If you have a better translation, it's "authority."

There are two Greek words for power, one is *ekousia:* it

means authority. The other is *dunamis:* it means power. And both words are used in this verse. "I give unto you power," literally "authority to tread on serpents and scorpions and over all the power"—and here it's a different Greek word, *dunamis*—"of the enemy: and nothing shall by any means hurt you."

Let me clarify these words by illustration. The word *authority* is actually a stronger word than the word *power.* You may have the power, strength, or ability to walk into my house and carry out my stereo. You say, "I have the power to do it." By that you mean you have the brute strength, the ability to get it out the door. But you don't have the authority. If you try it, I'll say, "What are you doing? You don't have the authority to take that out of here." So you see that authority is actually greater than power.

Another illustration: Envision a semi-truck loaded down with steel bars, roaring down a highway at sixty-five miles per hour. It represents *dunamis* (power): that is brute power, tons of weight. Then a little man weighing about one hundred and fifty pounds, wearing a blue uniform and a badge, steps out in front of that truck. He blows his whistle and puts up his hand; and the truck stops. The policeman had *ekousia*—authority. The physical power of the semi-truck is subject to the authority of the policeman.

Our English word *dynamite* is a derivation of *dunamis.* Luke 10:19 literally translated is, "I give you authority over all the dynamite of the devil." Hallelujah! If Jesus has given us authority over the devil, there is no reason to be frightened of him.

"I am in authority here," is what the believing Christian should quote in all confidence to the devil.

A man in Salina, Kansas, who received the baptism in the Holy Spirit under my ministry, related this incident to me. One night his wife awakened gagging, choking, and coughing. She had a persistent tickle in her throat and could get no relief. The husband awakened to the commotion with the anointing of the Holy Ghost upon him. He sat up in bed and delivered a mighty message in tongues. The interpretation of the tongue quickly followed, again through him, "Satan, I'm head of this house; and you let my wife go!" When he said that, the coughing tickle immediately left. That is divine authority. A husband can pray for his wife better than anyone else— better than any preacher. Because he, in God's order, is in direct authority over his wife and children. We need to use our God-given authority.

"I will give you authority," Jesus said.

"Really, Lord?"

"Yes, I give you authority."

"Over what, Lord?"

"OVER ALL..."

"*All,* is that what it says?"

"Over all the power of the enemy, and nothing shall by any means hurt you."

"Nothing, Lord?"

"*Nothing* shall by any means hurt you."

I believe that verse. I have faith in the authority of that verse and in the authority of Jesus. Faith is, of course, as vital to deliverance as it is to any other area of the Christian life. And yet, the devil will very cunningly try to corrupt even the concept of faith. It is essential that all in the deliverance ministry and all those who seek deliverance be aware of the danger of *negative faith.* I believe an incident in which a well-known Bible teacher, Derek Prince, was ministering will clearly illustrate this perversion of true faith.

As he was praying for a lady after a service, Derek laid his hand on her head and said, "Sister, I see a cloud; and that means you have been involved in the occult."

"Why," she said, "I've never messed around with that."

"Have you ever been to a fortuneteller?" he asked.

"No."

"Palm reader?"

"No."

"Seance?"

"No."

"Spiritualist?"

"No," she said, "I would never have anything to do with that sort of thing. I have never had any association with the occult, or spiritualism, or fortunetelling."

"Well, Lady," he said, "I'm not the Holy Ghost. I might be wrong. Let me pray for some other people." He did and he came back the second time. He laid his hand on her head and said, "I see that cloud. And every time I see that cloud it means that somewhere you've been into divination."

The lady insisted, "I've never been to a palm reader or a fortuneteller or anything like that."

Derek said, "Can you come back tomorrow night?"

She said, "Yes, I can."

He said, "You go home and ask Jesus what that is that I am seeing."

She came back the next night and said, "Derek, Jesus showed me. When I was pregnant with my first child, at the altar rail of the church after the morning service, the most 'spiritual' woman in our church came up to me. She said, 'Let me read your palm.' And standing there in front of the church after the morning service, she said, 'Your baby will be born dead.' When my baby was born, the cord was wrapped around its neck four times and it was strangled to death. The doctor told me that the cord is not long enough to wrap around the baby's neck more than twice, it is a very rare thing for it to be wrapped around twice, and three is unheard of. He just did not understand it. Nevertheless, it was wrapped around the baby's neck four times."

Derek looked her right in the eye and said, "Because you believed what the handmaiden of the devil told you, you gave him authority over you, and the devil killed your baby. That is *negative faith*. That is faith in the wrong direction. That is faith in the kingdom of darkness. It is faith in Satan, instead of in the Lord Jesus."

When I heard him say that, I recognized a principle. The principle is: *fear is faith*. If you fear that you are going to get cancer, you are believing that you are going to get cancer. If you fear that you're going to have a car accident, you're believing that you're going to have a car accident. That is faith in the devil. That is faith in darkness. That is faith in the words and power of the enemy which is directly contrary to this verse of Scripture: "I give you authority over all the power of the enemy, and nothing shall by any means hurt you."

By way of comment to the incident related above, let me underline the fact that every one of you who has ever had his palm read or been to a fortuneteller needs deliverance from the devil. Don't tell me, "Well, I didn't mean it, because it was just for fun and I didn't believe it." When you went to the handmaiden of the devil, you opened yourself up to a demon, and your depression and suicidal tendencies are a direct result of it. You cannot submit yourself to a handmaiden of the devil and come away free, regardless of what your motive was. And don't say, "Well, it happened when I was sixteen, and now I'm sixty." Do you know what that means? It means that you've had forty-four years of torment because of it and it's time for you to be freed. It doesn't make any difference what age you were.

While I was participating in a deliverance meeting in a hotel in Jerusalem, someone said to me, "You'd better not cast out devils. They will make your wife sick. Those demons will make your children or your wife sick back in Kansas City."

I said, "I don't believe it."

If I had believed it, the devil would have made them sick because I would have given him the right and privilege and authority to get at my family by my faith in him. If Jesus can't protect my children six thousand miles across the sea, it would have been a weak Jesus I was serving. You don't need to worry like that. It is nothing but devilish propaganda.

Faith in the devil is a bummer. You go through two-thirds or half of your life and you don't even know that demons are real. Then one day you hear about demons, and for the first time you say, "My goodness! These little demons are real and I have one of them." And the *backlash of deliverance* is that you then begin to believe in them. And when you believe in them, you give them authority over you. Because you have faith in them, you end up in a new type of spiritual difficulty.

I don't *believe* in demons. (Notice my verb.) I know they exist. I know they are real, but I don't have faith *in* them. I believe they exist, but I don't believe they can harm, hurt, or bother me. Do you see the difference?

Recently I was in Warrensburg at Central Missouri State College. A Catholic nun, Spirit-filled, and a Spirit-filled Episcopalian priest had a deliverance meeting with a brother there who was, as a result, set free. Subsequently, however, the backlash came. He went home and began to get thoughts like this, "I wonder if I am really free?" He began to doubt. He began to believe that the demons could bother him. He began to gag and to choke, then he began to cough, and became extremely upset emotionally. He was frantic.

I was in a meeting with the college students in the afternoon. About five thirty the Episcopalian priest came to me and said, "Brother Gruen, could you come help us? This brother is freaked out; he is gagging and choking.

His mother is upset. We don't know what to do." So away we went.

I walked into the house, and saw him lying across the bed, breathing heavily and with great difficulty. Everyone said, "Look! Look! We don't know what to do."

I said, "In the name of Jesus sit up. In Jesus' name sit up and get hold of yourself!" and he sat up.

I said, "I want to show you a verse." He began to act up again. I said, "In the name of Jesus I want you to read this verse." I turned him to this verse, "I give you authority over all the power of the devil, over all the power of the enemy and nothing shall by any means hurt you." I said, "Brother, read it out loud."

He read it, "I give you authority over snakes and scorpions and over all the power of the enemy and nothing shall by any means hurt you."

I said, "Brother, read it again."

The third time he read it, he said, "Over ALL the power of the enemy."

I said, "Read it again." He read it the fourth time and he began to laugh. I said, "Brother, read it again." The fifth time he read it I said, "Brother, you've had too much faith in the devil. He can't hurt you. Is that verse true?"

He said, "Yes, it is." And he was free! Free in five minutes time. I repeat, he was free in five minutes time!

Why was he free? Because, "If you know the truth, the truth shall set you free." I showed him the truth. The truth is, "I give you authority over all the power of the enemy and nothing shall by any means hurt you."

A brother in a certain city came to me. He had cast demons out of hundreds, and even thousands throughout the country. He is a good brother, a sweet brother. He said, "They crawl all over my arms. They give me heart pains. I can feel them. I can even feel them giving me headaches and they make me sick."

I said, "Brother, I don't believe it."

He said, "Don't they do that to you?"

I said, "No, I don't believe in it." (Are you catching the principle of negative faith?)

He said, "Well, why do they do that to me?"

I said, "Because you believe that they can do that to you. You've got too much faith in the devil."

The next day I was going to the radio station to deliver a tape and my head started hurting. I said, "Satan, I don't believe in it," and it left. Then I had a pain in my heart and I said, "I don't believe that either." When it left, I started getting nauseous. I said, "I don't believe that either," and it left. You are in sad shape if you have faith in Satan instead of faith in Jesus.

The principle of negative faith applies to healing as well as deliverance. A lady came to our church and said, "Brother Gruen, I've got diabetes, leukemia, and digestive trouble up and down my entire digestive tract."

I looked her right in the eye and said, "I don't believe it." I wasn't calling her a liar. She had faith in that sickness, and I put my faith squarely against her faith. If she believed in leukemia, the devil would do her the favor of giving it to her. I said, "Let's pray." I laid my hand on her head and said, "God, fill her full of unbelief..." Her eyes came open and began to blink like a toad in a hailstorm. Then I finished my sentence and said, "Fill her full of unbelief in her sickness."

How in the world can you believe in your sickness and believe in Jesus to heal you at the same time? You cannot walk north and south at the same time, and you can't believe you are dying of leukemia and that Jesus is your Healer at the same time. *You can't believe in two directions at the same time.* I had her pray this prayer:

"Lord Jesus, with Your blood, wash away all my faith in this leukemia." (The only thing that can remove negative faith from you is His blood.) "With Your blood wash away this diabetes, and with Your blood, wash away my faith in this digestive trouble. I renounce my faith in this sickness. I repent of it. Amen." Thereafter, I rebuked the sicknesses and commanded them to leave her.

I said, "I'm going to show you a verse and I want to know if you will obey this verse."

She said, "I will obey the Scriptures."

"Now," I said, "before I show you this verse, I want to tell you this—if you obey this Scripture, you will live; but if you don't you will die."

"Well," she said, "I'll keep it."

Three times I repeated that her life would depend upon obedience to this one verse. "What's the verse?" she asked. "I'll do what it says."

I turned her to Isaiah 33:24: "The inhabitants shall not say, I am sick."

If she had gone out of there saying, "I am sick, I've got leukemia," she would have died. That woman is still alive and she doesn't have leukemia. That has been over two years ago. She has no diabetes and she has no digestive trouble. But if she had gone out saying, "I'm sick, I'm sick," it would have been like Job, who said, "For the thing which I greatly feared is come upon me, and that which I was afraid of is come unto me" (Job 3:25).

Do you see that fear is negative faith—faith in the devil? How in the world can you ever get healed of arthritis or sinusitis if you believe you have to keep it? I don't believe in sinusitis or arthritis. Hallelujah! You can be healed right now because Jesus Christ will set you free. You can't believe in hay fever and Jesus at the same time.

The trouble with many people—and I say this kindly— is that they have too much faith in the devil and in sickness. Let's suppose we have a deliverance meeting and many are set free. I don't want you going out believing in the demons. Many people act as if the demons sit on the eaves of the church and when they leave the meeting and walk underneath the eaves, the demons say, "Whee!" and jump back on them! It does not happen in that way at all.

Let's say that you get rid of an unclean spirit such as lust or fornication or masturbation. If you go to an X-rated movie, you'll get the demon back. But it won't be the devil's fault—it's your fault because you chose to willfully transgress in sin. And it won't be "the devil made me do it." You did it and because you opened the door, the demon came back; but that demon cannot come back into you unless you deliberately choose to sin and live in it, rather than repent. The demon won't even come back in you if you repent of the sin.

Take a spirit of bitterness, for instance. Some new wound occurs and we are tempted to be bitter again. If we will kneel down and pray that thing through and ask the blood to cleanse the bitterness out of us, there is no way that spirit can get back in us. But, if by an *act* and a *choice* of our will, we choose not to forgive someone and choose to be bitter; yes, we will get the spirit of bitterness back. But it won't be the devil's fault. It will be our fault because by a choice and a decision that we made inside ourselves, we opened the door to him again. You don't have to worry about something like a demon getting up some morning and saying, "Hey, there's ole Joe. Let's jump him." It doesn't work that way. We have to open the door; and it's because of *our* choice and *our* sin that a spirit can come back.

Do you fully understand? We must become free of faith in the devil. I want you to fully comprehend the principle of negative faith as I did when I heard Derek Prince say, "You believed in what the handmaiden of the devil said, and because you believed it, you gave Satan authority over you."

You may wonder why a demon desires to enter a human being. The reason is that a demon wants a body through which to manifest his personality, a body yielded to emanate his wicked, ungodly, filthy nature.

But the Holy Spirit, the Spirit of Jesus Christ, also wants a body through which to manifest the personality of Jesus. "What! know ye not that your body is the temple of the Holy Ghost?" (1 Corinthians 6:19). The Holy Spirit desires that every one of us be just like Jesus Christ. He wants all to be a manifestation of Jesus Christ in their homes. He wants us fathers to be a manifestation of Jesus Christ to our wives and our children.

If I asked the wife of any Christian, "Is it hard for you to submit to your husband?" that wife should be able to say, "No, because my husband treats me like Jesus Christ would, and it is not hard to submit to that." The Bible says, "Husbands, love your wives as Christ also loved the church and gave himself for it." Do you know what that means? He is saying, "Husbands, treat your wives like I treated you when I was hanging on the cross for you."

The fruit of the Holy Spirit, according to Galatians 5:22, 23 is love, joy, peace, long-suffering, gentleness, goodness, faith, meekness, and temperance (self-control). And the seed is in the fruit. Where is the seed of an apple?—it's in the fruit. Where is the seed of a peach?—it's in the fruit. God hasn't called you men to be your wife's personal preacher. He has called you to love her. And He hasn't called you wives to be your husband's personal chaplain. He has called you to be your husband's helpmate. The seed is in the fruit. More important than anything you say is whether you manifest *love* and *joy* and *peace* and *gentleness* and *patience* and *goodness, faith* and *meekness* and *self-control*. If others can see that kind of fruit, they'll want it. If your husband sees gentleness and patience and joy and peace and meekness and self-control (particularly of the tongue) in you, do you know what? He's going to take a big bite of that fruit and he's going to swallow some seed.

The seed is not in the gifts, but in the fruit. If you are sweet, everyone around you will want Jesus Christ. They will line up to knock at your door to get it. "I don't agree with some of her convictions. But I'll say one thing, she is surely a sweet person." You've won. They swallowed some seed when they took a bite out of your life.

So often we are prone to be harsh and judgmental. "Are you saved, brother? If you're not, *you're going to hell.*" Many times an approach like that is nothing but the flesh and it profits nothing. Start being gentle, start being like Jesus. If you begin acting like Jesus, everyone around you will be saved because they will want the life that you manifest.

Most Christians are victims of what I call the "gunnysack effect." If you were a prizefighter and entered the ring with a gunnysack on your head, you'd get beat to a pulp. The bell rings, your opponent begins punching, but you can't hit him—you have no idea who or where he is. The average Christian has no idea what temptation is. If you were tempted with the thought to commit adultery, you would immediately know it was of the devil, and you would command, "Satan, get out of here in Jesus' name." The same devil can come with many other types of temptations and you might not even realize that it is the enemy. In the next chapter I will give a detailed explanation of how Satan tempts us through our thought life. The thought realm is the arena of Satanic attack.

Ephesians 6:12 tells us that "We wrestle not against flesh and blood, but against principalities, against powers, against the rulers of the darkness of this world, against spiritual wickedness in high places." Demons seek to pervade and pervert our whole realm of life. We desperately need to remove the gunnysack concerning other less recognizable areas of demonic activity.

Most people can be bitter or resentful without it ever occurring to them that it is a demon; but if not dealt with properly, that attitude can get hold of a person and control his life.

Have you ever considered worry as sin? And yet worry is the opposite of peace and faith. Why worry? Let God do your worrying for you! If the Prince of Peace resides within you, there is no room for worry. But if you don't recognize worry as temptation, you continue in it, not realizing that the devil has you without your knowledge. Take off the gunnysack!

In America violence is more of a problem in many ways than sex. We are a generation of violence because we see so much. The average child in the five-year span between the ages of nine and fourteen sees 14,000 murders on television! We cannot watch 14,000 murders, many of them horrifyingly explicit in detail and shocking in depravity, without it doing something to our spirits. It destroys our sensitivity. When I saw the movie *The Cross and the Switchblade*, I was really grieved. I realize it was a good movie for the world, but it grieved the Holy Spirit inside me. I couldn't stand the violence. I can see how a worldly person could see that movie, be brought under conviction, and as a result get saved. I would not condemn it in the least; I am simply pointing out that with exposure to so much violence, the tenderness leaves one's spirit.

The realm of demonic activity is not confined to "worldly" places. It may be hard to accept the idea of demons in a church, but there is scriptural precedent for it in Mark 1:23, "And there was in their synagogue a man with an unclean spirit, and he cried out." When somebody cries out and interrupts a service, it is always a demon. That is the wrong spirit, the spirit of rebellion; it is not submissiveness, it is not meekness, it is not the Holy Spirit. The Holy Spirit is a Gentle One. If someone screams in our church, he'll be rebuked; we'll cast the devil out of him. The Holy Spirit doesn't interrupt a man when he is preaching, under the anointing. Too often the Holy Spirit is blamed for the work of demons. (A tragedy which hinders many from receiving the baptism in the Holy Spirit).

One day we were singing and worshiping, and all of a sudden a lady screamed out, and the whole church instantly became silent. They all knew it was a demon, and they all looked up to the platform to see what I would do as she was screaming out in tongues. But it was a counterfeit spirit speaking in tongues. When you ask the Father for the Holy Spirit in the name of Jesus, you can't get any counterfeit. But this woman had been to a spiritualist meeting, and whenever you delve into the occult, spiritualism, and seances, you are very likely to get a counterfeit.

As she was screaming out in tongues, the Lord said to me, "Just keep praising Jesus." So we resumed singing. We sang a little bit longer and she screamed twice, she screamed three times, and then the Holy Spirit went through me like a bolt of lightning. A tongue came out of me with the interpretation right after it, "Come unto me saith the Lord and I'll set you free." Then both the tongue and interpretation were repeated. The woman rose and made her way down the aisle as I called for the elders. We gathered around her.

"Do you want these demons cast out of you?" I asked.

She said, "I sure do."

We commanded, "Satan, let her go in Jesus' name." With a piercing scream they left her. Then I continued, "How would you like to receive salvation through Jesus?"

70

She said, "I do want to be saved." We led her to Jesus, she repented, asked the blood to cleanse her, and invited Jesus to come inside her.

Now I said, "How would you like to receive the baptism in the Holy Spirit?"

She said, "I sure would."

We said, "Receive ye the fullness of the Holy Spirit," and a very gentle, quiet, beautiful language came from her and she was full of the Holy Spirit. The first language had been harsh and critical, even the intonation of it was demonic.

I've heard some say, "Bless God, just stick to the fruit, brother, because Satan can counterfeit the gifts—but he can't counterfeit love." That is a very naive statement. Have you ever seen counterfeit love? I have. Have you ever seen counterfeit joy? I have. Have you ever seen counterfeit peace? I have. Satan can imitate any fruit of the Spirit or any gift of the Spirit.

Consider self-control: I've seen people who thought they had self-control, when actually they were under legalistic religious bondage. It wasn't self-control at all, it was a counterfeit of self-control. The devil does show up at church!

In agony of spirit, I have sat through lectures by seminary professors who state, "We know that Jesus just used this form of language to accommodate Himself to the culture and customs of His day." With one swing of the pen, they completely negate the words of Jesus Christ. If the Lord Jesus was casting out demons, you'd better pray twice before stating it is not real; you are putting yourself in the place of saying you're smarter than Jesus. As for me, I'll line my theology up with Jesus Christ. I believe the Son of God was right.

Let's continue with the account of the evil spirit in the synagogue in Mark 1:23, "And he cried out, saying, what have we to do with thee, thou Jesus of Nazareth?" Notice that demons nearly always travel in groups. This demon crying out of the person in the synagogue objects, "What have *we* to do with thee?"

I have found it nearly always true that if someone has a demon of lust, he also has a woman-hating spirit. Or if it is a woman, a man-hating spirit. They are usually accompanied by a spirit of seduction, and frequently masturbation. Here is a group of four kindred spirits. So when we rebuke spirits, we must always rebuke the entire group. In the case of depression I have found it necessary to renounce depression, despondency, discouragement, disillusionment, hopelessness, and suicide. One lets in the other, and they nurture each other. I've had visions of one demon holding on to the ankle of the other demon helping it to stay in the person.

"What have we to do with thee, Jesus of Nazareth? Art thou come to destroy us?" An account in Matthew records a demon asking, "Art thou come to torment us before our time?" Hell is real. If you don't believe in hell, you know less than the devil. The devil knew he was eventually going to hell and he complained to Jesus. "Have you come early? We aren't supposed to get cast into there yet. Have you come to torment us before our time?" Don't let yourself be deceived by the devil into thinking hell is simply a mythological figment of someone's imagination. It is a reality awaiting the devil and his children (see John 8:44).

The demon said to Jesus, "I know thee who thou art, the Holy One of God." Demons know who Jesus is. They acknowledge His holiness. If you are holy, they'll know who *you* are, too. But you're kidding yourself if you say you are *full* of the Holy Spirit and you have lust and hate in you. I received a letter from a college group who said they were filled with the Spirit but they still smoked dope. The polarity of that statement should be clear to any

Christian. Or, if you have dirty, filthy, lustful thoughts in your heart and mind all afternoon, you're not *full* of the Holy Spirit, regardless of whether or not you speak in tongues. If you have hate for your mother-in-law, you're not *full* of the Holy Spirit.

"Jesus rebuked him saying, Hold thy peace and come out of him." Jesus refused to talk to demons. Early in my ministry, I did talk to them, but I don't do it any more. It is scriptural to command them to give their name, but that is all. Even in exorcism or deliverance, if you talk to demons, you're actually one step away from spiritualism, because you're consulting demons for advice and counsel. You cannot trust what they tell you unless you have them really bound tight and know what you're doing. And if you know what you're doing, you don't talk to demons. Scripturally we should not speak to demons, we should say, "Hold your peace. Come out of him."

After Jesus had commanded him, "The unclean spirit, tearing him; and crying with a loud voice, came out of him." Demons come out in various ways. Sometimes they will scream or throw a person to the floor. We must not be astonished at these manifestations should they occur; however, as discussed earlier, this need not be a prolonged process, but merely a momentary manifestation as they depart. Prolonged manifestation indicates a need for repentance and reading of the Word.

Many times, also, demons will leave without apparent notice. A little 5-year-old girl who had never been to our church before, came up to me after a Thursday morning Bible study and said, "I've got an earache."

I said, "You earache, I command you in Jesus' name, let her go." Then I asked, "Is it gone?"

She said, "Yes, it is."

Afterward, while having lunch with a friend, the girl's mother asked skeptically, "How's your ear, honey?"

"Well," she said, "Jesus healed it."

The friend asked, "Where did the pain go?"

The little girl replied, "Right out of my mouth." The spirit left through her mouth. The Greek word for spirit is *Pneuma:* wind, breath, or spirit. Usually they come out of one's mouth.

An infant daughter of a deacon in Topeka had several severe food allergies. There was only one milk formula the baby could tolerate and the only food she could take by spoon was vegetables. After the Wednesday night service, the local pastor and I went by to minister to the baby. I laid hands on her and said, "You allergies, loose this baby and let her go." Amazing as it may seem, the baby burped. The spirits left. The next morning the mother put the baby on homogenized milk and started feeding her cereal. She showed no ill effects at all.

This first chapter of Mark records the great excitement in the synagogues when the demons bowed to Jesus' name. "They were all amazed, insomuch that they questioned among themselves, saying, What thing is this? what new doctrine is this? for with authority commandeth he even the unclean spirits, and they do obey him...and at even, when the sun did set, they brought unto him all that were diseased, and then that were possessed with devils...and he healed many that were sick with divers diseases, cast out many devils and *suffered not the devils to speak;* because they knew him...and he preached in their synagogues throughout all of Galilee, and cast out devils." This isn't a new doctrine. It comes right out of the Bible which is as old as Jesus' ministry is. Now if Jesus did it, why in the world aren't we doing it today?

How do you get rid of an evil spirit? You don't treat a devil with kindness. You don't say in a meek and fearful voice, "Devil, will you please leave?" If you went home and found somebody in your house who didn't belong there, you'd tell him to leave on no uncertain terms. You've got to tell the devil where to go and how long to stay. You are a temple of the Holy Spirit and the demon is a trespasser. It is on God's property.

Just because you're saved doesn't mean you're immune to temptation. Salvation doesn't provide immunity from satanic attack. Without a battle there is no victory.

I don't believe a Christian can be demon possessed. Possession indicates total ownership. A Christian can have a spirit, but the spirit doesn't have him completely in the sense of demon possession. Therefore, since that spirit is a trespasser, you must take your stand against it. It's that simple.

Demons are serious business. You cannot play games with them; you must tell them to leave.

The summary of the ministry of our Lord is recorded in Acts 10:38: "God anointed Jesus of Nazareth with the Holy Ghost and with power; who went about doing good, and healing all that were oppressed of the devil; for God was with him." We are not off base if we go about doing good and healing all that are oppressed of the devil, anointed with power and the Holy Ghost; we're following Jesus.

CHAPTER

4

Thought Control

The thought realm is the great arena of temptation in which we are either defeated or victorious. How do thoughts get into our minds. Where do they come from?

Thoughts can come from three sources: the Holy Spirit, evil spirits, or our senses. Stimuli to any of the physical senses—sight, hearing, touch, smell, taste—can cause thoughts to come into our minds. Obviously if I stick your arm with a pin, it will run a sensation to your spinal column, then to your brain, then back again, and that will create thoughts. But, those thoughts originate from your physical senses.

Unless we consider the question of how thoughts enter the mind, we will inevitably be under condemnation. Satan can give us thoughts of the wildest, most perverse, ungodly nature, but it's important to understand that they don't come from us.

Several years ago, as I was casting a demon out of a person, the demon began to rebel, "I like it here, I'm staying. You can't cast me out; this is my home and I'm staying."

I said to that demon, "In the name of Jesus Christ I command you to tell me how you got hold of this woman." (This was done in my early ministry.)

The demon flippantly answered, "Through thought-impartation."

I asked, "What do you mean, 'thought-impartation?' Tell me the truth in Jesus' name."

The demon answered, "We drop our thoughts into her mind."

I asked, "What kind of thoughts? Tell me the truth in Jesus' name."

The demon replied, "Thoughts of murder, adultery."

I asked, "What other kind of thoughts? Tell me the truth in Jesus' name."

And the demon replied in a tone of chilling defiance, "To break the ten commandments."

Satan tries to get hold of our mind and behavior through dropping his thoughts into our minds. We must realize that just because it came *to* us doesn't mean it came *from* us. Many thoughts which come into our minds come from evil spirits.

One lady my wife and I prayed with was convinced that she was a computer. She said, "They have me programmed, they know everything I'm doing. Don't tell me it's not true because someone will walk up to me at work and tell me exactly what I'm thinking. They've got it all programmed; I am just a computer and somebody else is pushing the buttons." She really believed it.

After about two hours of prayer and teaching, finally, she saw the light and said in an astonished voice, "You mean these thoughts I have don't come from me? You mean I am not a computer?"

My wife said, "Yes, that's what we've been trying to tell you. Those thoughts are not coming from inside of you, they are being dropped into your mind by a demon."

She was set completely free when she realized those thoughts weren't hers. That has been three years ago and she is still free.

In a sense, demons can be good news. When you realize that filthy, ungodly thoughts aren't from you, but from a devil, that is a great relief. And, praise God, there is a way to handle those thoughts.

Hebrews 4:13-15 states, "Neither is there any creature that is not manifest in his sight: but all things are naked and open unto the eyes of him with whom we have to do. Seeing then that we have a great high priest, that has passed into the heavens, Jesus the Son of God, let us hold fast our profession. For we have not a high priest which cannot be touched with the feeling of our infirmities; but was in all points tempted like as we are, yet without sin." Imagine! Jesus Christ was tempted in all points like as we are, yet without sin. Every type of thought that you have had, whether fear, confusion, depression, self-condemnation, even unclean thoughts, Jesus Christ experienced, but He didn't yield to them, He didn't say, "Yes" to them. He didn't agree with them. They were repulsive to Him.

So often we are blindly deceived by the devil, who drops a thought into our mind, then condemns us by saying, "Why are you thinking that? Look how wicked you are, look how bad you are." In other words, he *gives* us the thought and then he hits *us* over the head with it. He billy-clubs us and says, "Look here, you're not sincere, you're not genuine, look at those thoughts you have." And yet *we* didn't even have them. Satan dropped them into our mind, then accused us because we had them.

We are brought under condemnation by believing the devil's accusations and then find ourselves assaulted with guilt thoughts, "If I'm a Christian, why was I thinking like that?"

The Bible says that Jesus was tempted in all points like we are. He can be touched with our infirmities, with feeling for our infirmities. He can feel what it's like to be a human, because although the Scriptures say he was the Son of God, yet the Son of God became flesh and lived in a body. He had the same mechanisms that we have and the same assault upon his thought life. Jesus Christ surely must have had some incredible thoughts thrown at him by the devil. Walking up that hill of Golgotha to be crucified, the devil undoubtedly was saying to him, "Those guys aren't worth dying for. They don't love you." He must have had a temptation of rejection and loneliness, indeed all kinds of temptations just as we have.

We can't help what thoughts come into our minds, but we *can* choose what to do with them after they get there. There is an old saying, "You can't keep the birds from flying over your head, but you can keep them from building a nest in your hair." We can't keep those thoughts from flying at us. Suppose all the thoughts that came into our minds were projected on a movie screen for our whole church to see. None of us would like that! But that really is not fair. The true revealer of our thought life would be a screen to show which thoughts we *yielded to,* cooperated with, said "yes" to, and built on.

If a thought comes into your mind which alarms and upsets you, that is your spirit and the Holy Spirit saying, "no" to it. You have not sinned; you have been tempted to sin, but you have refused the temptation. It is very important to understand the sharp distinction between being tempted to sin and sinning.

We need to be aware of the characteristics of thoughts which come from the Holy Spirit, from ourselves, and from demons. One day God spoke to me and said, "Make a list of the fruit of the Holy Spirit and write down opposites for each one. You will have a list of demonic thought patterns. Let me introduce the chart which I made. I am sure you could improve on it, using your own insights and vocabulary. *It is meant to only be suggestive.*

THOUGHT-CONTROL

Scriptures: Psalm 34:6-7; Prov. 23:7; 1 Cor. 6:19-20; 1 Cor. 10:13; 2 Cor. 10:4-5; Gal. 5:22-23; Eph. 6:11-12; Phil. 4:8-9; Heb. 4:13-15; 1 Peter 5:8-9; 1 John 1:7-9

Holy Spirit Thoughts	Demon Thoughts	Demon Habits	Demon Control
Love	-unforgiveness -resentment -bitterness -jealousy, hurts	Hatred	Murder
Joy	-depression -despair -discouragement -disillusionment	Hopelessness	Suicide
Peace	-nerves, tension -worry, fretting -confusion -restlessness	Fear	Nervous Breakdown
Longsuffering	-impatience -selfishness -disharmony -annoyance, temper	Wrath	Violence
Gentleness	-harshness, cruelty -inconsideration -arguing -jealousy	Unreasonableness	Insanity
Goodness	-filthy thoughts -evil imaginations -pornography -flirting, seduction -masturbation	Immorality (fornication)	Perversity
Faith	-doubt, hesitation -anxiety -indecision -negative faith -backsliding	Agnosticism (Atheism)	Blasphemy against the Holy Spirit
Meekness	-pride -self-ego -self-exaltation -dissensions, disunity -unteachable spirit	Domination	Witchcraft
Self-Control (temperance)	-drunkenness, dope -gluttony -gossip, slander maniac, depression -compulsive behavior -hypnosis	Emotional Instability	Maniac
Holy Spirit Fruit	Rulers	Powers	Principalities

The first column I have labeled *Holy Spirit Thoughts* because any thought which agrees with the fruit of the Holy Spirit, comes from the Holy Spirit. For example: If your child has accidentally broken the living room window and you suddenly feel a flood of compassion and love for him, you know that is the Holy Spirit speaking to you in your mind to be longsuffering or gentle. If you get a thought of faith, that comes from God. A thought to be meek, not to be self-asserting, not to lift yourself up, that's from the Holy Spirit. Any thought which agrees with the ninefold fruit of the Holy Spirit obviously comes from the Holy Spirit.

Column Two I have labeled *Demon Thoughts;* column Three, *Demon Habits;* and column Four, *Demon Control.*

There is definitely a hierarchy that is controlled by the devil. Ephesians 6:12 tells us that "We wrestle not against flesh and blood, but against principalities, against powers, against rulers of the darkness of this world, against spiritual wickedness in high places." Here is outlined at least a threefold panorama of satanic power. Notice it says, "We don't wrestle against flesh and blood"—it's not your dad, it's not your mom, it's not your neighbor, it's not your preacher, it's not your school teacher, it's not your natural brother or sister, but it's the powers of darkness. Your husband is not the problem; the battle is in the heavenly realm with the spirits. These columns opposite the fruit of the Holy Spirit comprise a list of satanic thought-patterns with which the devil would like to trick you.

As we examine this chart in detail, it is clear that Satan tries very subtly and gradually to control our thought-pattern to the point of gross sin. What is the opposite of love? Unforgiveness, resentment, bitterness, jealousy, *all of which leads* to something worse—hatred, which leads ultimately, to the principality called murder.

The opposite of joy might begin with something as mild (in our eyes) as slight depression, yet that can lead to hopelessness and eventually suicide.

Have you ever considered worry as sin? And yet the opposite of peace is worry, which can lead to fear, and the devil's ultimate goal for you—nervous breakdown.

The opposite of longsuffering is impatience, anger, disharmony, selfishness—which lead to wrath. The real reason that we are impatient is that we are selfish. We become easily irritated if someone fouls up our schedule, our plans, our what-we-want-to-do. But if it is God's day, God's schedule, it can't be fouled up. We forget that, then we get provoked because the phone rings, or someone comes unexpectedly, or the kids won't get on the ball and snap to it, or the wife takes too long to get dressed. The root of impatience is selfishness, which leads in its final consequence to violence.

The opposite of gentleness is harshness, or arguing, or not being considerate. It leads to a very serious consequence, unreasonableness. The final result is a person totally insane—demon-controlled.

The opposite of goodness includes filthy thoughts, evil imaginations, pornography, flirting, seduction, which leads to immorality, which leads ultimately to the worst kinds of perversity.

The opposite of faith is doubt, hesitation, worry, anxiety, indecision, or secondguessing a decision. These could lead to agnosticism or atheism, and to me the ultimate conclusion of unbelief is blasphemy of the Holy Spirit. That's how serious unbelief is. In one sense, unbelief is the most serious sin of all, causing a denial even of the work of God in you. The root of all backsliding is unbelief.

Pride and all of its attendant characteristics comprise the opposite of meekness. These include self-ego, self-exultation, selfish ambition, dissensions, disunity, and an unteachable spirit. These easily progress to domination, wanting to control people or events, which is the basis of witchcraft. Witchcraft is the attempt to control a person or circumstance, by any spirit other than the Holy Spirit.

Lack of self-control can be manifested in many ways: drunkenness, dope, gluttony, slander (the tongue is the most unruly member), emotional instability. The tongue needs desperately to be controlled. So do the emotions. Many, many people are manic-depressive to some degree. One day they are "on top of the world," the next day they have a case of the "blahs." Jesus Christ is the *same* yesterday, today, and forever. Yet, it is not enough that Jesus is the same yesterday, today, forever. He wants to be the same in *us* each day. *The mark of a mature Christian is sameness!* Emotional instability leads ultimately to a complete loss of control and a maniacal personality.

Remember, one of the primary objections to taking dope is that it produces loss of control. Personally, I don't want to do anything that takes away from my free will or my ability to control myself and my actions. Anything which produces loss of self-control; drugs, liquor, hypnosis, etc., is extremely dangerous.

Totaling the three columns of demon thoughts, demon habits, and demon control, we have a total of sixty-nine different temptations that can come to you in the thought realm. Usually, upon mention of an ungodly thought, a person's first reaction is that it refers to one thing—lust. But we have seen that doubt is as dirty as a thought of lust, and a thought of depression is just as satanic as an unclean thought. Indeed, Satan has at least sixty-nine areas or categories in which he can wage war against us.

You can wake up in the morning, and sit up on your bed and rub your eyes. It looks cloudy and dismal, and you say, "I don't know, I just feel blah today; I just feel kind of depressed."

Stop the camera! Take a closer look. What happened right then was that Satan threw a thought into your mind to be depressed and you accepted it *without even knowing you were being tempted.* One of the reasons God's people are so defeated is that they yield to temptation so often without being aware of it. Be on the alert!

You know what you should say sitting on that bed? "Satan, you're a liar! Jesus is in me and I have His joy—*that*'s the *truth!* I don't care what my emotions say or what my thoughts are, I've got the joy of the Lord." Speak it with your mouth and you'll have the victory; you'll overcome.

The devil will usually speak to us in *the first person rather than the second person.* He's not going to say to us, "You are depressed, you are discouraged, you are despondant." If he did, we would catch on. He will nearly always speak to us in the first person, with the word "I," in order to trick us into despair, doubt, or whatever, as in the example above.

Ephesians 6:11 admonishes us to "put on the whole armor of God, that you may be able to stand against the *wiles* of the devil;" he is primarily tricky in the thought realm. The devil loves to get you in the mind game. Suppose you rebuke the devil six hundred eighty two times a day. Here comes a thought..."In the name of Jesus get out,"...it returns..."In the name of Jesus I rebuke you." Then follows the pattern thought ...rebuke...thought...rebuke. By the end of the day, I can imagine one demon turning to another demon and saying, "Well, he didn't sin, but *he still thought about us all day."* And the devil still won!

One of the best ways to overcome Satan is by evasion; simply ignore him. We can choose with our will what we want to think about. *Most people believe they are controlled by their mind;* but we don't have to be *governed by* our thoughts, we can *govern* our thoughts. We don't have to let our minds control us, *we can control our minds.*

"The peace of God, which passeth all understanding shall keep your hearts and *minds* through Christ Jesus. Finally brethren whatsoever things are true, whatsoever things are honest, whatsoever things are just, whatsoever things are pure, whatsoever things are lovely, whatsoever things are of good report; if there be any virtue, if there be any praise, *think on these things*" (Philippians 4:7-8). It would be ridiculous for God to tell us to think on these things if it were impossible for us to do so. The very fact that God says, "Listen, here are eight things to think about," means that it has to be possible for us to do it. We can choose what we want to think about. By the way, these eight things are a perfect description of our Lord Jesus.

Do you remember the Bible says there was a hedge around Job? I believe that the hedge is Psalm 34:6 and 7. "This poor man cried, and the Lord heard him, and saved him out of all his troubles. The angel of the Lord encampeth round about them that fear him, and delivereth them." Most of our troubles are mental troubles, mind troubles, thought troubles. As long as we don't receive them as coming from us, we won't suffer from them. We're nervous because we believe we're nervous. We must change our confession. We should say, "Hallelujah, I've got the Prince of Peace in me and I'm not nervous. Satan, you liar, get out of here in Jesus' name."

Do you realize that the angel of the Lord encamps round about them that fear the Lord and delivers them? Now if we have an angel as our hedge, that's good news! Many times I pray and I ask God for angelic help. If I were sore oppressed in a certain area of my life, whether concerning despondency and despair, uncleanness, or perhaps self-ego and pride, I'd say, "God, You said Your angels encamp round about those who fear You and You deliver them, and I need an angel to pitch a tent right next to my mind and deliver me." God will supernaturally give us supernatural help. We don't have to have our minds as an open field that demons can trod across and use as a playground. We can have a fence and a wall as a protection. Our mind is not to be a garbage can. Hallelujah!

"What! know ye not that your body is the temple of the Holy Ghost?" In other words our body and everything our body contains belongs to the Holy Spirit. Comparing it to the architecture of the physical temple in Jerusalem, the outer court corresponds to our physical body, the Holy place is our mind, and the Holy of Holies is our spirit. We don't need to accept any demon or demonic thoughts in our holy place, in our mind.

There isn't one of us that is exempt from some demonic thought flowing toward us. Some of our temptations are a little different, but the Scriptures say, "The same afflictions are accomplished in the brethren," and "There hath no temptation taken you but such as is common to man." What is *un*common is someone who won't agree with them, who won't yield to them, someone who says "no" to those thoughts.

There are some people who almost tempt themselves. They begin the day by saying, "I'm not going to be depressed today...I'm not going to be depressed today...I'm not going to be depressed today..." And already they're depressed. Some of us have been "patsies" to the devil for years in a certain area of our personality. One demon turns to another demon and says, "We don't need to switch tricks, he's fallen for the same attack for eighteen years, we might as well keep it up. He believes he's depressed, so we have him." Our best bet would be to say, "Devil, I don't believe it."

Many times I don't even honor the devil with a rebuke;

I simply say, "I'm not interested in that." I don't believe Jesus went around rebuking the devil all day. *I believe He went around listening to the Father,* (John 5:17,19,30; 8:26,28,29,47; 14:10).

The Bible says that we are to cast down "imaginations and every high thing that exalts itself against the knowledge of God" and that we are to bring every thought into captivity "to the obedience of Christ" (2 Corinthians 10:5).

Five Ways to Resist Satan

There are basically five ways to resist Satan. "Resist the devil and he will flee from you."

The first is to quote Scripture like Jesus did during his forty-day wilderness temptation.

The second is to openly rebuke Satan. It is only recorded that Jesus did this one time—when Peter suggested that He need not go to the cross.

A third way is by praying in the spirit, namely, in the supernatural prayer language of tongues.

A fourth way is to learn to be rebellious—rebellious to Satan. Do exactly the opposite of what he is tempting you to do. One sister in our church literally baked a cake for a sister who Satan tempted her to resent.

But the height of resistance is silence. Simply ignoring the absurdity of the thoughts which come to us. Suppose my wife wanted to resist me. The deepest and most total resistance would be to absolutely refuse to talk to me. Nothing is more final than silence. When we refuse to even talk to the devil he says, "Rats, I can't even get him to talk to me." Silence and simply ignoring the thoughts which come to us is a very practical and effective way to resist Satan and live in victory in our thought life!

CHAPTER

5

Frontal Attack

"Now therefore fear the Lord and serve Him in sincerity and in truth; and put away the gods that your fathers served beyond the River and in Egypt; and serve the Lord. And if it is disagreeable in your sight to serve the Lord, choose for yourselves today whom you will serve; whether the gods which your fathers served which were beyond the river or the gods of the Amorites, in whose land you're living; but as for me and my house, we will serve the Lord" (Joshua 24:14 *NASB*).

The Lord, by revelation, quickened this passage to me as I was reading it several months ago. I was shocked to see the admonition, "Choose between me and the gods on the other side of the river" (the Euphrates). In other words, Joshua posed the same question years ago that every one of us face today: whether we're going to serve God, or serve Eastern religions. The gods on the other side of the river include almost everything from Buddhism and Confucianism to Sun Moon and Guru Mahara-ji. Joshua doesn't say, "Choose *what* you will serve," but "Choose *whom* you will serve." The deathbed appeal of Joshua as he goes off the scene is, "You choose which god you're going to serve, but as for me and my house, we'll serve Jehovah, we'll serve the Lord." It is clear that a choice must be made between God and false gods.

Very little is mentioned from pulpits or from the

Church concerning idolatory, but it occurs to me that the first commandment, "Thou shalt have no other gods beside me," is really the essential problem today facing the world. If we keep the first commandment, we really keep them all. We shall not have any other gods beside the Lord our God.

In a way, the number one god that you have is *you*. Sometimes I don't really think God cares so much what brand of sin we're into; what upsets God is that *we* are running our lives instead of letting Him have control. Really, the problem comes back to *our* choice, not demons. We are masters of ourselves. Joshua says, "*You* choose." The reference is to serving idols or Eastern religions, or serving God; but the real point is that *the choice is ours*. The number one idol is still wanting to run ourselves instead of turning the lordship of our lives over to Jesus Christ.

God has much to say concerning various forms of the occult. (A list of Scriptures against the occult practices will be found in the appendix.) The first verse of Scripture I want to consider is Exodus 22:18: "You shall not allow a sorcerer to live." In the Old Testament, the crime of practicing witchcraft or sorcery was punishable by capital punishment, by death. If you had walked down the street of a Palestinian village and seen a sign with a palm on it, it wouldn't have been long before you would have witnessed a stoning right on the spot. In Bible times, if there had been a Junior High School with a woman teaching communication, and on the communications bulletin board a palm showing how to tell fortunes by palm reading (this situation occurred in my own children's Junior High), that woman would have been stoned. Sorcery was so serious then that capital punishment was decreed by God.

Leviticus 19:26, "You shall not eat anything with the

blood, nor practice divination or sooth saying" *(NASB)*. You may think I'm carrying this too far, but because of this verse I have an aversion to rare steak, and you couldn't get me to touch blood pudding. To God, blood is holy, because the life is in the blood and blood was given for atonement.

Verse 31 of the same chapter reads, "Do not turn to mediums or spiritists, do not seek them out to be defiled by them: I am the Lord your God." In other words, God says we'll be defiled—mentally, spiritually, and physically—if we turn to mediums. I've prayed for people whose children were born with every allergy and physical problem imaginable after their parents had gone to a fortuneteller. Anyone who goes to a spiritualist gets defiled. When a person can't be freed of depression and suicidal tendencies, I always ask them, "Have you ever had your fortune told? Have you ever been to a spiritualist? Have you been to a séance?" Nearly always the answer is, "Yes, I have." That is the cause of the depression and sadness. You cannot get away with it; you will be defiled.

God states emphatically in this verse, "I am the Lord your God." In other words, what are you doing messing around asking demons for advice? I like to think of Jesus Christ waiting for me every morning in a private appointment in which He volunteers to be my wonderful Counselor. If you need advice, counsel or direction, the Bible says the Holy Spirit will show you things to come. Let Him quicken to your heart anything you *need* to know about the future.

What are you doing running to horoscopes for advice? Why don't you run to the Book? Why in the world is a saint going to demons for advice? The horoscope in the paper is a word from Satan for you for that day, and I surely wouldn't pay any attention to it. You can get a lot of fear and satanic advice by reading the horoscopes. Don't think for a minute that it's "just for fun." I've heard many people say, "Oh, well, I don't really believe it; it's just sort of like reading Peanuts, you know." I tell you something, the column in one of our local papers is written by a professional witch who, by her own testimony, got her gifts from a gypsy fortuneteller. When you read what she writes for your "sign," it is inspired by the devil, and it's demonic advice. Even the reading of it causes it to get into your spirit to some extent. You had better leave it alone.

Leviticus 20:6 and 7 reads, "As for the person who turns to mediums and to spiritists, to play the harlot after them, I will also set my face against that person and will cut him off from among his people. You shall consecrate yourselves therefore and be holy, for I am the Lord your God" *(NASB)*. Here God says that if we go to a medium or to spiritists, we are playing the harlot. King James says, we're going whoring after other gods. It is a serious thing when God calls somebody a whore or a harlot or a prostitute. Spiritually speaking, if we go to a spiritualist, we are a harlot or a whore, and we're practicing prostitution—not of our body, but of our spirit. We are putting our spirit, the deepest part of us, in union with a spirit other than the Holy Spirit. We are committing spiritual adultery! God doesn't like that, and God says, "I'll set my face against you and I'll cut you off from among the people." If we choose other gods and if we choose to put our human spirit in union with an evil spirit or a demon, God is against us. People ask why their prayers aren't answered: this is one reason. People wonder why God doesn't bless their lives. One reason is that they have other gods: God doesn't like idolatry. He will not put up with competition. It is impossible to get anywhere with God if you have been into spiritualism, divination, astral projection, hypnosis, a follower of Edgar Cayce, or any of these types of things unless you repent, renounce it, turn from it, and call it what God calls it: spiritual adultery! We must say what Joshua said, "I'm done with and I forsake other gods. I choose for me and my household to serve you, God, and no other." The Bible says in one place, "I'm a jealous God." God wants to be the one and only sweetheart, or Groom. For you to have your fortune told is spiritual adultery. It is that serious. You are going whoring after other gods, committing the exact sin which destroyed Israel. This is why they went into captivity, and you will go into captivity also as a result of dealing in the occult.

Spiritualism, fortunetelling, and divination can destroy America. Some of our leading presidents in times past had spiritualists as their counselors. One of them, after he was counseled by a spiritualist, gave away half of the world to Communism and then died in office. We need a president and leaders that go to God, not to witches, sorcerers, and spiritualists for advice. This is one thing you should diligently pray about.

Leviticus 20:27 states, "As for a man or a woman, if there is a medium or a spiritist among them, they shall surely be put to death; they shall be stoned with stones; their bloodguiltiness is upon them" *(NASB)*. From the literal Hebrew the idea of this verse is a man or a woman who has a ghost or a familiar spirit *within him* or *operating through him*. So, in other words, if you had approached a Hebrew and announced, "I've got ESP," he would have said, "Where is the rock pile?" By openly claiming to foretell the future, or stating he had a spirit (other than the Spirit of God), a person was destined for capital punishment.

Astrology and horoscopes are becoming increasingly popular today as forms of amusement or parlor games in addition to those who take them more seriously. Hear the Word of the Lord concerning these things: "Beware lest you lift up your eyes to heaven and see the sun and the moon and the stars, all the host of heaven, and be drawn away and worship them and serve them, those which the Lord your God has alloted to all the peoples under the whole heaven" (Deuteronomy 4:19 *NASB*). This scripture states a clear warning against the worship of stars or the host of heaven.

Isaiah 47:11-14a tells the consequences of those who fall into this sin. "But evil will come on you which you will not know how to charm away; and disaster will fall on you for which you cannot atone; And destruction about which you do not know will come on you suddenly. Stand fast now in your spells and in your many sorceries with which you labored from your youth; Perhaps you'll be able to profit, perhaps you may cause trembling. You are wearied with your many counsels. Let now the astrologers, those who prophesy by the stars, those who predict by the new moons, stand up and save you from what will come upon you. Behold, they've become like stubble, fire burns them; They cannot deliver themselves from the power of the flame" *(NASB)*. Here, Isaiah is mocking. He says that judgment is coming, but what good are all your monthly prognosticators? They are like the stubble of the wheat field; the fire is going to burn them up and there will not be any to save them. "Stand up with all your astrologers and false prophets and all of your diviners, they're not going to save you now," Isaiah soberly warns.

Jeremiah 8:1-2, a passage concerning the worship of stars and making prognostication by the stars and the moon, states, "'At that time,' declares the Lord, 'they will bring out the bones of the kings of Judah, and the bones of its princes, and the bones of the priests, and the bones of the prophets, and the bones of the inhabitants of

Jerusalem from their graves. And they will spread them out to the sun, the moon, and to all the host of heaven, which they have loved, and which they have served, and which they've gone after, and which they've long sought, and which they have worshiped. They will not be gathered or buried; they will be as dung on the face of the ground" (NASB).

Now that is really a graphic prophecy! What is going to happen to all these prophets and kings and priests and leaders who worshiped the sun and who looked to the moon and the stars for counsel and advice? The judgment of God will fall. They're going to lay out underneath the same sun, moon, and stars; and they're going to be unburied and their human flesh is going to rot underneath their false gods; they're going to become manure and fertilizer for the ground. I imagine Jeremiah wasn't too popular, but Jesus said, "Woe unto you if all men speak well of you for so did they the false prophets." Well, I can't think of any prophecy that puts it any more clearly than that.

You may have wondered about the fact that some of these occult people tell prophecies which later come true. What about that? Deuteronomy 13:1 provides the answer: "If a prophet or a dreamer of dreams arises among you and gives you a sign or a wonder, and the sign or the wonder comes true, concerning which he spoke to you, saying 'Let us go after other gods (whom you have not known) and let us serve them,' you shall not listen to the words of that prophet or that dreamer of dreams; for the Lord your God is testing you to find out if you love the Lord your God with all your heart and with all your soul. You shall follow the Lord your God and fear Him; and you shall keep His commandments, listen to His voice, serve Him, and cling to Him. But that prophet or that dreamer of dreams shall be put to death, because he has counseled rebellion. [literally, "turning aside"] against the Lord your God who brought you from the land of Egypt and redeemed you from the house of slavery, to seduce you from the way in which the Lord your God commanded you to walk. So shall you purge the evil from among you" *(NASB)*.

The test of a prophet isn't always that his prophecy comes true. Here the Scriptures clearly teach that sometimes a false prophet or a dreamer of dreams does foretell the future. How can that be? It's very simple. *A demon can prophesy the devil's plans.* I have noticed that people who are into fortunetelling, divination, or that sort of thing, always prophesy death, accidents, divorce and tragedies of various types. They nearly always deal in negative prophecies. They speak of death instead of life. Demons communicate back and forth and they love to prophesy to you that you're going to get a divorce. As you believe it, you start having trouble and a divorce actually results. But the Scriptures say that just because someone with a demon prophesies something that happens, you haven't justification to follow them: *don't do it!* In fact, it says they should be put to death!

Several years ago, a nationally known prophetess prophesied seven feet of snow for Kansas City. I thanked the Lord that I knew what to pray against, and I said, "You foul spirit that would bring a snowstorm on this city which would paralyze it with seven feet of snow, I bind you in the name of Jesus." I trust that other Christians bound that spirit, too. That year only three or four inches of snow fell all winter long.

There is a psuedo-charismatic group which operates a so-called Bible college, including a course entitled "Visions and Caskets" dealing with visions of people in caskets. Frank McLaughlin and I happened to be used of God in rescuing one of the young persons who had been tricked into that situation. We had never seen anything so demonized in all of our lives. When we hear prophecies of that type or hear of visions of a destructive nature, we can take authority over them in the name of Jesus. We should thank God that we know what to pray against because the devil has tipped his hand by such means.

God issues a safeguard against false accusations in Deuteronomy chapter 17. Verses 2 thru 5 declare that any man or woman guilty of the abomination of worshiping or serving false gods, especially the sun, moon, and any of the heavenly host, be stoned to death. However, verses 6 and 7 state that stoning be carried out only upon the evidence of two or three witnesses and those witnesses are to throw the first rock. God's method would certainly eliminate most false accusers of witchcraft.

A summary of various types of occultism is found in Deuteronomy 18:9: "When thou art come into the land which the Lord thy God giveth thee, thou shalt not learn to do after the abominations of those nations. There shall not be found among you anyone that maketh his son or his daughter to pass through the fire (as in a sacrifice) or that useth divination, or an observer of times, or an enchanter, or a witch, or a charmer, or a consulter with familiar spirits, or a wizard, or a necromancer. For all that do these things are an abomination unto the Lord: and because of these abominations the Lord thy God doth drive them out from before thee."

The Old Testament passages which I have quoted in this chapter give an absolute prohibition against all types of the occult—from horoscopes to necromancing (a necromancer is a person who consults the dead to try to bring them back for advice; in other words, a spiritualist.)

Likewise, the New Testament fully concurs concerning the occult. Galatians 5:19 clearly states, "Now the deeds of the flesh are evident, which are: immorality, impurity, sensuality, idolatry, sorcery...I forewarn you just as I have forewarned you that those who practice such things *shall not inherit the kingdom of God" (NASB)*.

Revelation 18:23 says, "All nations were deceived by your sorcery." Revelation 21:8 tells the fearful end of all those who practice such abominations, "but the fearful and unbelieving and abominable and murderers and whoremongers and sorcerers and idolaters and all liars, shall have their part in the lake that burns with fire and brimstone: which is the second death." Revelation 22:15, speaking of the holy city, new Jerusalem, states, "*Outside* are the dogs and the sorcerers and the immoral persons and the murderers and the idolaters and everyone who loves and practices lying" *(NASB)*.

The interesting thing about these passages is the use of the Greek word *pharmaceia* from which we get the word *pharmacy*. It literally means the employment of drugs for the purpose of enchantment, sorcery, or magic. The Greek indicates a definite connection between the use of drugs and the occult. We should have realized with the advent of a drug culture that a Satan worship culture would naturally follow, because it is all tied up in this word *pharmaceia*.

The form *pharmacos,* one who deals drugs, is used in Revelation 21:8 and 22:15. A drug dealer shall have his part in the lake which burns with fire...outside are the dogs, the idolaters, and the drug dealers, an enchanter, a magician or a sorcerer.

Drugs and the occult are serious business. Perhaps you're not interested in this subject, but you may have nieces or children or grandchildren involved—or some lady next door who invites you over for coffee and wants to get you into ESP or Edgar Cayce or shows you her Zodiac tablecloth. It's relevant to us today regardless of our position or age level.

Let's return for a moment to the subject of necromancy or spiritualism. 1 Samuel 28 records an interesting, and to some, a puzzling account of King Saul consulting a necromancer, the witch of Endor. Saul was living in sin and disobedience and, as a result, he had lost contact with God. The Bible says he inquired of the Lord, but God wouldn't answer him, either by dreams or by prophets. So he decided to inquire of a witch. Perhaps the reason many people go to spiritualists is that they are backslidden, don't know how to pray and are not right with God, so they go looking to a fortuneteller for advice. Everyone wants to know what's going to happen. If they're not in communication with God, they may seek supernatural knowledge from demonic sources. You may wonder, then, why sorcery is listed with the works of the flesh when obviously it's a demon: simply because of the human quality inherent in the old nature—curiosity about the future. And, of course, the old nature seeks out sorcery to provide the supernatural instead of Jesus Christ, holiness, and God, since it's not interested in going God's route.

King Saul disguised himself and approached the witch of Endor. After extracting a promise of secrecy concerning the encounter (since Saul himself had ordered the death penalty for known witches), she asked whom he wanted her to contact. He replied, "I want Samuel." Samuel had just died. The interesting thing is that when Samuel showed up, it scared that witch half to death. She cried out in shock and amazement that it worked. Samuel asked, "What are you bothering me for?" He continued, "My only message to you, Saul, is that you rejected God and tomorrow you're going to be where I am. Your children, also. You are going to die." That wasn't a very pleasant message for Saul, but it did happen and it should be a stern warning to us to never become involved in the slightest with a witch or a spiritualist. "So Saul died for his trespasses which he committed against the Lord, because of the word of the Lord which he did not keep; *and also because he asked counsel of the medium making inquiry of it and did not inquire of the Lord.* Therefore He killed him and turned the kingdom to David, the son of Jesse" (1 Chronicles 10:13 *NASB, italics added*).

This verse also backs up the contention that those who go to spiritualists end up depressed and suicidal. Actually Saul tried to kill himself. I've watched for it and after praying with hundreds and hundreds of people who have been in the occult, I have observed that every one of them has been depressed and suicidal.

The devil is using spiritualism in our day in a particularly insidious way to infiltrate the Church, even the charismatic renewal. It is a definite possibility that the whore church (the false church) will not come out of modernism as many believe, but the harlot will come out of spiritualism. The devil is trying to make spiritualism appear religious and pious. The only thing that can possibly get the harlot church together is a spirit. The same principle is true with the Bride. The only thing that's been able to bring true believers together is the Holy Spirit. In the same way the harlot church will be brought together by a spirit. Church counsels or committees will never be able to accomplish this union. It will take an evil spirit to bring together the whore church. I believe that it will be built around the worship of some female deity. Please notice that in Revelation 17 the whore church is pictured as a woman riding the beast or the anti-christ. The concept of a female deity or mother worship is not something new. Second Kings 17:16-18 lists this very sin among those committed by Israel against the Lord— "And they forsook all the commandments of the Lord their God, and made for themselves molten images, even two calfs, and made an Asherah" [a wooden symbol of a female deity], "and worshiped all the host of heaven" [their horoscopes] "and served Baal" [who is also a fertility god]. "They made their sons and their daughters pass through the fire, and practiced divination and enchantments, and sold themselves to do evil in the sight of the Lord, provoking Him. So, the Lord was very angry with Israel, and removed them from His sight; None was left except the tribe of Judah" *(NASB)*.

It is very important that the reader understand that idolatry is really spiritual adultery. Adultery is allowing your body to be put in union with someone else's body (other than your mate's). Idolatry is allowing your spirit to be put in union with another spirit *other than the spirit of Jesus*. Idolatry, therefore, is worse than physical adultery, because it is adultery of your spirit. God views idolatry seriously and always brought severe judgment upon its practice—as any casual reader of the Old Testament will realize, the entire nation of Israel was wiped out because of idolatry or spiritual whoredom. Their idolatry is even described as "going a whoring after other gods."

This also applies to the Rapture of the Church. I see the Rapture like this: Jesus coming in the clouds and the Holy Spirit emanating from Jesus to the earth. At this point, everyone with the same spirit—*zap*—is caught up to meet Him in the air. But here are Mr. and Mrs. X, or Sister Y, and Brother Z who are still half-committed to this and half-committed to that, playing religious games and committing spiritual adultery. When the Spirit of Jesus goes out to grab them, there is no *zap* because they have a different spirit . . . the spirit of whoredom. They have two gods. They're not part of the Bride, but of the whore church, because they have two husbands. This is serious: only those who have the Holy Spirit will be caught up. Church members will not necessarily be caught up, nor preachers, nor non-denominational "Christians," nor your denomination. Only those who know Jesus Christ as Lord, and who have the Holy Spirit as their spirit will meet Him in the air.

The problem in America is most definitely not a one-man problem; it's not political; our national leaders are only a reflection of the spiritual condition of our nation. The problem in America is the worship of all kinds of gods other than Jesus Christ. The problem reaches into every village, every city, every farm—to you and to me.

We should contemplate with fear and trembling the fact that Israel was destroyed for the very sins which we see rising daily in America. When you understand that God has no respect of nations, then you realize that we're doomed if we don't get rid of our other gods. Every fortuneteller is an enemy of America. Every horoscope column is a curse on this land and a potential source of destruction. The current craze for movies on the occult and exorcism is an abomiantion to God and a stench in His nostrils.

Acts 19:11-20 illustrates the consequence of trying to "invoke" the name of Jesus without really knowing Him. "And God wrought special miracles by the hands of Paul: so that from his body were brought unto the sick handkerchiefs or aprons, and the diseases departed from them, and the evil spirits went out of them. Then certain of the vagabond Jews, exorcists, took upon them to call over them which had evil spirits the name of the Lord Jesus, saying, We adjure you by Jesus whom Paul preacheth. And there were seven sons of one Sceva, a Jew, and chief of the priests, which did so. And the evil spirit answered and said, Jesus I know, and Paul I know; but who are ye?" [The Greek is quite emphatic in this question, because two Greek words for "to know" are used. Literally translated, the emphasis is, "I'm well acquainted with Jesus and I've had some dealings with Paul, but who in the world are you?"] "And the man in whom the evil spirit was leaped on them, and overcame them, and prevailed against them, so that they fled out of that house naked and wounded. And this was known to all the Jews and Greeks also dwelling at Ephesus; and fear fell on them all, and the name of the Lord Jesus was magnified. And many that believed came, and confessed, and showed their deeds. Many of them also which used curious arts brought their books together, and burned them before all men: and they counted the price of them, and found it fifty thousand pieces of silver. So mightily grew the word of God and prevailed."

People began to recognize that the Scriptures, the Word of the Lord, had dominion instead of witchcraft books. It is amazing that the bonfire totaled fifty thousand dollars worth of occult books. People have said to me, "I can't throw away my occult books. I've got three hundred dollars worth of them." Well, praise the Lord, you could just have a three hundred dollar bonfire.

For a number of years I had a book by a prophetess on my shelf. When we moved to this church, I put it in my pastor's study, rationalizing, "Well, I'm a pastor and I don't believe it. It won't bother me, but I'll keep it as a reference to show people that she's of the devil." But, its presence kept weighing on my mind. One morning I happened to be reading in Deuteronomy when the book came to my mind again. I just quit reading and looked up and said, "Lord, I know the passage about the bonfire in Acts, but if you really want me to get rid of that book, I want you to show me in another verse of Scripture besides that one." To my surprise, about ten verses later I read in Deuteronomy 7:25,26, "Get the accursed thing out of your house." God said, "You've got it in *My* house." That was my answer and a few minutes later I was out in front of my garbage can, ripping up the book. The Holy Spirit made me burn it.

If you want to be completely free, you've got to get the accursed thing out of your house. This includes every statue, every occult book, all the occult literature, ESP books, hypnosis books, Edgar Cayce, astral projection— you know what they are if you're into them. These things can be openings for attacks on your whole family. If you're not willing to go home and have a bonfire, you're playing games. It must be a total rejection of all other gods. "Thou shalt love the Lord thy God, and *Him only shalt thou serve.*"

Let me say that caution must be exercised when burning occult literature. People in my church as well as all over the country have testified that when they burned their occult books, the fire leaped out of the incinerator and all kinds of supernatural things happened. I know of one family whose entire back yard was burned. Stand out there with a hose and burn carefully. I don't mean that as a joke. You are dealing with demons and they are real beings who really hate you.

There is a brother in our church who was into the occult before he got saved and delivered. He said something to me that I consider precious and I want to share it as a concluding remark. He said, "Ernie, when I gave my heart to Jesus Christ, it was a total commitment. The way that God showed me that all those other things were wrong was that I couldn't totally commit myself to them. Oh, I went to an Edgar Cayce study group, and I studied the books some, but it wasn't there. I couldn't give myself totally, I couldn't turn myself absolutely over to it—it just wasn't there."

There is one person that you can totally commit yourself to, to whom you can turn over your family, your life, your possessions and your money, your mind, your spirit, your body, everything. That one person is Jesus Christ. And that's what it means to be a Christian—to *totally* commit yourself to Jesus as your Lord, as your only God.

CHAPTER

6

What Is Reality?

Satan loves religiosity. Satan is in the "church-building" business. Since Satan is a counterfeiter, religion is one of his favorites. While the occult is the frontal attack of demons, Satan loves a subtle attack from the rear, as well. I believe that religious spirits can cheat us out of a real walk with Jesus—out of a vital, personal relationship with Him. In one sense, we must beware of "religion" even more than sin—because of its subtlety. The distinction between "religion" and reality is of such vital importance to the Christian walk that we must examine this ray of truth together.

Most people think their basic choice is between sin and holiness; between serving Satan and serving God. However, there are really three options available to us: sin, "religion," or Jesus. Many people get into "religion" without entering into a real, vital, personal relationship with Jesus Christ, hearing the voice of Jesus for themselves, being led by the Holy Spirit. They would rather have a *rule;* then, they can follow the rule. They don't have to think; they don't have to pray. "My group says so-and-so"—and that's their rule; that's their doctrine; that's their human teaching. Those individuals don't get into the Word for themselves; they don't have a real relationship with Jesus. Instead, they have a relationship with a law or with a rule, which many times involves demonic religious bondage.

I want to share here a shocking testimony from the Leavenworth Penitentiary that helped open my eyes, spiritually, on this subject:

"I came back to Jesus, my Lord and Savior, just ten months ago. But in just that short time, I have seen so much 'form of godliness, which denies the power thereof'—even here in Leavenworth Penitentiary—that there are times that I feel like I went from 'organized crime' to 'organized religion.' I'm beginning to feel like there are two Mafias...'organized crime,' the 'Little Mafia,' and 'organized religion,' the 'Big Mafia.' The organized criminals ignored Jesus, but it was organized religion which said: 'Crucify Him!'"

Just consider that: from organized crime to organized religion. I've found it intensely difficult, personally, to define in my own heart and understanding the difference between religion and Jesus. It's easy to say, "Well, religion is going to church, shaking a preacher's hand, being water-baptized, but not having Christ." But it's more complex and involved than that. Joining the church without being saved is just one small illustration of being religious.

One night, in a matter of a few hours as I meditated, God gave me a chart showing twelve ways to understand the difference between religion and what I will call *reality*. By *reality*, I mean *the real presence of Jesus*. Hallelujah! You could say, the difference between religion and presence; the difference between religion and really having Jesus Christ's presence with you, in you, guiding you.

The first question that came to me (and I call these "key issues" in the first lefthand column of the chart) was: *Who is Lord?* Religion makes a law the lord. But, on the other hand, *reality* makes Jesus Christ Lord. Now let me share with you the first verse of Scripture, Colossians 2:19-23:

"And not holding fast to the Head, from whom the entire

108

	KEY ISSUES	RELIGION	REALITY	SCRIPTURE	ILLUSTRATIONS
1	Who is Lord?	A Law, Laws or Rules	Jesus Christ	Col. 2:19-23, Rom. 7:4-5, 1 Cor. 15:56	No need to think, Pray, Search. Television (Matt. 6:22-23, Col. 3:2)
2	Motivation	(Temporary) Obligation, Duty	(Permanent) Love, Enjoyment, Want To	John 14:15, Gal. 2:20	Family Devotions, Prayer Life
3	What Spirit Is In Control?	Spirit of Bondage (Slavery)	Holy Spirit	Rom. 8:15	Schedules, Fasting
4	Authority	Tradition of Elders, Human Teaching (Phariseeism)	New Testament (Discipleship)	Mark 7:1-23, 2 Tim. 3:16-17, James 1:25	Homosexuality, Fornication, Hair
5	End Result	Dead Works	Fruit of the Holy Spirit	Heb. 6:1, 9:14, Gal. 5:22-23	Hospital Call
6	Source	Soul, Flesh	Holy Spirit	John 6:63, Heb. 4:12	Witnessing, Worship
7	Attitude	Self-Righteousness, Pride, Judging	Secret Prayer, Patience	Luke 18:9-14, Matt. 6:6	Nagging is the opposite of prayer
8	Future Slant	Institutionalization of the Past, Status Quo	Glorious Liberty	Rom. 8:14, 21	Church Bulletin, Liturgy
9	Focus	Do's and Don'ts	Love for Jesus Christ	1 Pet. 3:3-4, Luke 10:27	Jewelry, Clothes
10	God's View	Abomination (Hate)	Delightful and Precious	Isaiah 1:10-20, Matt. 23:13-33	Degrees of Sin
11	Mental or Spiritual Condition	Inner Guilt, Anxiety	Rest	Heb. 4:1-11	You will never find a happy legalist.
12	Method of Salvation	Works/Law	Faith/Grace	Eph. 2:8-10, Rom. 10:1-11, Gal. 2:16, 3:11-12	False Spirit of Repentence
	Summary	Bad News	Good News	Rom. 10:15	

body, being supplied and held together by the joints and ligaments, grows with a growth which is from God. If you have died with Christ to the elementary principles of the world, why, as if you were living in the world, do you submit yourself to decrees, such as, 'Do not handle, do not taste, do not touch!' (which all refer to things destined to perish with the using)—in accordance with the *commandments and teachings of men?* These are matters which have, to be sure, the *appearance of wisdom* in *self-made religion* and self-abasement and severe treatment of the body, but are of *no value against fleshly indulgence. (NASB italics added).*

Notice, he says they don't hold fast to the Head; that is, they begin to preach other things besides Jesus. They revert to man-made religion and submit to legalistic human decrees, such as "do not handle, taste, or touch." But—their old natures do not change—they remain the same inside! They change externally, but not inwardly. Their religious rules have "no value against fleshly indulgence."

Let's take television for an example. I know that God revealed to me the dangers of what television can do to the spiritual life of people. In Matthew's Gospel, the phrase "Repent, for the kingdom of God is at hand" is repeatedly used. The word "repent" means to change your mind. Much of today's television programming "changes your mind" to think like the world, instead of "changing your mind" to think like Jesus or the Word of God. Therefore, the person who spends a lot of time watching routine television programs has his mind changed to the opposite of what Jesus wants. Television becomes the opposite of repentance. Standard television programming is often satanic brainwashing—having your mind *reworlded* instead of *renewed.* Again Jesus said, in Matthew 6:22-23:

"The lamp of the body is the eye; if therefore your eye is clear, your whole body will be full of light. But if your eye is bad, your whole body will be full of darkness. If therefore the light that is in you is darkness, how great is the darkness!" *(NASB)*

From this verse we can see the danger of having our eyes looking at regular television programming. The end result will be bodies full of darkness, and the destruction of the family unit. It is like having an open sewer flowing into the corner of the living room!

"Set your mind on the things above, not on the things that are on earth" (Colossians 3:2 *NASB*).

But wait a minute—I got a real revelation from God, and what happened next? I noticed my spirit beginning to change, and I began to become self-righteous, critical, and religious. *Read carefully*. We can receive a revelation from God, only to have Satan pervert it. Consider, for example, Jesus' temptation in the Wilderness. Who put him on that forty-day fast? The Holy Spirit did! This was the very fast with which Jesus Christ began His public ministry—getting alone with God for forty days to get clear instruction from heaven. And what did the devil do? He said, "See that rock there, Jesus? Turn it into bread!" In other words—now catch this—Satan took a situation that God had ordained and tried to twist it into a temptation. Do you see that? Do you understand?

Suppose you have a real, godly love for a brother or sister—a deep admiration and respect. Well, Satan's desire is to twist that beautiful thing into lust. Satan will try to pervert anything that is good and holy. Satan tried to pervert my revelation on the dangers of television—how? By getting me to start preaching religion: "If you have a television, you're sinning!" The result is a human decree—a law: that's religion. "If you watch any television at all, you're sinning!" I ask: where is that rule in the Bible? Such teaching is a step backwards to a rule, or to a law, or to religion. If the television issue, for instance, is boiled down to a neat rule, then we no longer need to pray; we don't have to ask or seek God, and we no longer are following the Lord. Our lifestyle falls into the pattern of the Pharisee. Equally dangerous is the fact that we do what Paul warned the Colossians against: we deny ourselves fleshly desires, but it doesn't do anything for us. In our hearts we're just as worldly as we ever were—still wanting it—still wishing we had it. But, because a spiritual leader says to get rid of it, we do so, keeping the seething inward desire.

God, however, looks on the heart, and He wants to do something deeper: *change the desire.* We could take the television out of the house and say, "We'll never watch it again!" with our heart's desire remaining absolutely the same—no change whatsoever. But we've obeyed the rule, so now we're religious. And God sees our heart—with the same problems, the same old nature, the same lack of victory—except now we have another problem: we think we're right with God because we kept a rule! "Do not touch. Do not taste. Do not handle." Who is the lord of a religionist? A rule; a law. Go to the Pharisee: he says, in effect, "My Lord is the Talmud." A rule or a law becomes Lord, instead of a person, *The Person,* Jesus Christ.

I preached a message once, entitled "Leviticus 28." As the congregation turned in their Bibles to the book of Leviticus they were astonished to find that there are only 27 chapters in Leviticus. The point of that message was that we who believe the Word of God do not subtract from Scripture, but rather, we often add to it. It's as much a sin to add to the Word of God as it is to subtract from it . . . and most of us have made a whole bunch of rules that make up our own individual Leviticus 28. The Bible says in Proverbs 30:6;

> "Do not add to these words, lest he reprove you, and you be proved a liar" *(NASB).*

Are we living under the law—Old Testament law? Of course not! We're saved by grace! But how about all the charismatic laws? Or the personal laws? The real danger for many Christians is not going back under the Old Testament laws, but coming underneath their own laws. People make all kinds of regulations and rules for themselves which they cannot keep. For example, one person states emphatically, "Aspirins are little white devil pills." Now where do you find *that* in the Bible? "It's Leviticus 28:17." Or, someone else says, "I must fast every Friday." You'll find that in the Bible, too—Leviticus 28:53. It's obvious that the list is endless. Every group in every area of the nation has a few of its own special rules that it adds to the Scriptures for its Leviticus 28 list.

Romans 7 says that we are dead to the law (verse 4) and we are married to another, Jesus Christ, who is raised from the dead ... which means, instead of checking with any church's rules or any man's rules, you check with *the Person—Jesus Christ*. In reference to television, Jesus would say "You can watch *this* program; you *can't* watch that one." So you're free to obey the Lord instead of a rule or a law or group of laws. Do you understand the principle? Television is merely an example. It's dangerous when you substitute pharisaical laws instead of *reality*— the reality of hearing His voice and seeking His face.

Let's say you're praying one day, and Jesus Christ your Lord says to you: "You know, that television is really hurting you and your wife." So you both feel quickened to get rid of it, and a change comes over your heart attitude. *Now* you get rid of it because you feel led of the Lord to get rid of it, and your heart's really in it, and the decision has done something for you.

Family after family have come to me and said, "My children's personalities completely change in half a day's time when they watch television." A college boy came to me and said, "Brother Ernie, since I've been home from college I haven't had victory in my Christian life. When you mentioned what you did about your television, it dawned on me that I've been saturated with television since being home, and I'm just not in the Spirit any more." It "dawned on him" by the power of the Holy Spirit; not by condemnatory laws or regulations. If you shut the television off, do it because Jesus Christ, by the Holy Spirit, has shown it to you, rather than some preacher setting up a rule that you have to obey. The self-righteousness that comes from obeying the rule is as bad or worse than the original problem, *when the rule is Lord instead of Jesus.* Religion will say, "Turn it off . . . period!" But *reality* lets each believer, as God's slave, be free to let Jesus Christ be his Lord in each situation—instead of being slaves to man's laws or revelations.

The second key issue listed in the chart is *Motivation.* Motivation. With religion, you do something because it's an obligation, a duty, "I gotta do it;" and, I put the word "temporary" there because if you're going to church out of duty or obligation, I tell you, it's a temporary thing! It won't last! Sooner or later, you'll drop by the wayside, and it'll probably be sooner! But, if it's "I love it, I enjoy it, I want to"—then, hallelujah! It'll be permanent; because, even if you drop by the wayside for a few Sundays, you'll say: "Oh, I loved it there, I love to worship, I love to hear the Word," and that love for Jesus will draw you right back to be into church, or into your private devotions, or whatever.

In the *Illustration* column, number 2, I list *Family Devotions.* The Saturday night when I read the letter from the brother about switching from organized crime to organized religion, I called all my family in and I said, "Let's get down on our knees and pray for the services tomorrow. Okay?" That was tremendous! Why did we do that? I felt led by the Holy Spirit to do it. So now it's Sunday morning, and we've just had a glorious time of blessing in the Lord, so I begin to issue new orders: "All right, from now on we forget our Saturday night prayer meetings, and all of you stay home every Saturday night, get down on your knees with your families and pray! That's right—pray, and pray some more, there at home with your families every Saturday night, all of you—" What happens? It becomes duty; then it's obligation; it's as dead as a doornail; in short, it's religion. Instead of telling you *that,* I tell you that when the Holy Spirit gives you a desire to pray with your family and it means something and it's not just a rule or duty or an obligation, but there's a real desire in your spirit to worship the Lord, well, it's better that way than to demand *"Six-thirty, come in here, kids!"* Nobody wants that, including the enforcer of the rule. It becomes fleshly; it becomes religion—why? Because the motivation is wrong in religion—completely different from the motivation of reality. When it's religion, we say "I'm *supposed* to go to church, so I'll go. We're *supposed* to have family devotions, so we'd better do it."

No, I tell you, "God is a Spirit, and they that worship Him must worship Him in spirit and in truth." If you go to church right now *only* because it's your duty, you're in trouble—real spiritual trouble. But, if you say, "Boy, I love it!"—then your motivation is right.

John 14:15 says, "If you love me you will keep my commandments." What's the problem? Why doesn't somebody keep the commandments or keep the New Testament? It's a motivation problem. They don't really love the Lord. The same thing applies to the prayer life: it's got to come from your heart. If the motivation is duty, you're slipping into religion instead of *reality.*

Key Issue Number Three: *What Spirit Is In Control?* Look at Romans 8:15:

"For you have not received a spirit of slavery leading to fear again, but you have received a spirit of adoption as

115

sons by which we cry out, 'Abba! Father!' The Spirit Himself bears witness with our spirit that we are children of God" *(NASB)*.

Illustration Number Three says *Schedules* and *Fasting*. Now, suppose you hear a sermon on fasting, and you know you ought to fast, and it should be a regular part of your Christian life. So, what do you do? You say, "All right, God from now on, I promise You, I even vow to You, that I'm going to fast every Friday." Do you know what happens next? You've got yourself under a spirit of bondage, and when you fast it's apt to do more damage than good . . . you'll be out of the Spirit the entire time you're fasting. Recently when I was fasting I was out of the Spirit, and I got so crabby and grouchy and mean that I would have been much better off not fasting. Ask my wife—she'll tell you. I hadn't been so unkind in a long time. There's something about the old nature that wants to get into bondage; there's even a desire to be in chains! Did you ever make schedules? I can remember when I made schedules in seminary . . . "God, I'm going to keep this, now—6 to 6:30 private devotions, 6:30 to 7:00 clean up, 8:00 to 8:50 this class, free hour study for that class—I couldn't ever keep one of those things! Did you ever do that? Schedules and promises and resolutions. It's just bondage, instead of letting the Holy Spirit tell you what to do and when.

Key Issue Number Four: *Authority.* For someone in religion, authority is the tradition of the elders—not just "Bible-times-elders," but tradition of the elders today: human teaching. Notice on the chart, I've put *Phariseeism* in parenthesis: the religious authority leads to Phariseeism; but *reality*'s authority is the Word of God, and the opposite of a Pharisee is a disciple. Man, I'm going to keep the whole Bible! If it's in the Bible, I'm going to keep it! You see, that's the heart of a disciple. Amen? Hallelujah!

116

Now I'd like to share Mark 7 with you—this is really an interesting chapter of Scripture:

And the Pharisees and some of the scribes gathered together around Him when they had come from Jerusalem, and had seen that some of His disciples were eating their bread with impure hands, that is, unwashed. (For the Pharisees and all the Jews do not eat unless they carefully wash their hands, thus observing the traditions of the elders; and when they come from the market place, they do not eat unless they cleanse themselves; and there are many other things which they have received in order to observe, such as the washing of cups and pitchers and copper pots.) And the Pharisees and the scribes asked Him, "Why do Your disciples not walk according to the tradition of the elders, but eat their bread with impure hands?"

Now—look at what Jesus said:

And He said unto them, "Rightly did Isaiah prophesy of you hypocrites, as it is written,

> 'THIS PEOPLE HONORS ME WITH THEIR LIPS, BUT THEIR HEART IS FAR AWAY FROM ME. 'BUT IN VAIN DO THEY WORSHIP ME, TEACHING AS DOCTRINES THE PRECEPTS OF MEN.'

"Neglecting the commandment of God, you hold to the tradition of men." He was also saying to them, "You nicely set aside the commandment of God in order to keep your tradition.

"For Moses said,

> 'HONOR YOUR FATHER AND YOUR MOTHER;'

and,

> 'HE WHO SPEAKS EVIL OF FATHER OR MOTHER, LET HIM BE PUT TO DEATH;'

but you say, 'If a man says to his father or his mother, anything of mine you might have been helped by is Corban (that is to say, given to God),'
you no longer permit him to do anything for his father or his mother;

thus invalidating the word of God by your tradition which you have handed down; and you do many such things like that."

Now skipping to verse 20:

And He was saying, "That which proceeds out of the man, that is what defiles the man.

"For from within, out of the heart of men, proceed the evil thoughts and fornications, thefts, murders, adulteries, deeds of coveting and wickedness, as well as deceit, sensuality, envy, slander, pride and foolishness.

"All these evil things proceed from within and defile the man" *(NASB).*

So it's very easy, you see, to get tangled up with nonessentials—straining at gnats and swallowing camels. And, yet, you can have within your heart all these things listed in verses 21 and 22: lust, stealing, murder, covetousness, wickedness, envy, slander, pride, foolishness. You see, it's possible to do all the external things and keep all the tradition of the elders, and yet, have it not be well with your soul at all. Amen? It's much more than just going to church—you can keep all the "thou-shalt-not's"—don't drink, don't smoke, don't dance, don't cuss—and have all kinds of hate in your heart, all kinds of lust in your heart, all kinds of impurity.

On the other hand, the authority for those who want *reality* is the Word of God. For example, we list *Homosexuality* and *Fornication* in the *Illustrations* column. The Bible says that those who do such things shall not inherit the kingdom of heaven. So, when it comes to something explicitly forbidden in Scripture, we accept that—not as a man-made law, but as the Word of God. If we're disciples, we come completely under that authority, and we're done with those things forever. The "unnecessary rules" we mentioned earlier have nothing to do with things that are explicitly forbidden in Scripture. In other words, we're not compromising with sin: if it's forbidden, it's sin and it's wrong and you can't do it—not if you're a disciple.

Now, I may step on a few toes: take hair, for example (*Illustrations* Number 4). The "Jesus people" have gotten into religion, too. They have standards of acceptance, rules, traditions—in short, their religion. Someone accepts Jesus, becomes a Jesus freak and adopts the hippie culture. That movement carries with it an aura of religion as strong as denominationalism. The accepted standard includes sloppy appearance, long hair, sandals, etc. Now suppose someone in that culture is suddenly exposed to this verse in the New Testament: "It's a shame for a man to have long hair." What is his response? If he's looking for *reality;* to be a disciple, seeking the Lord in his life, he'll want to conform to a deliberate statement of God's preference for a man. However, if he's into the religious spirit of that movement, he'll discount that verse of Scripture, saying, "Oh, well, it doesn't really mean that; you have to consider the context of contemporary culture in Paul's day, etc.," and instead, he'll comply with the standards and rules of his "religion."

Key Issues Number Five: *End Result.* Notice the contrast—the end result of religion is dead works; the end result of *reality* is the fruit of the Holy Spirit. Hallelujah! Hebrews 6:1 says that we should repent from (turn away from) dead works...and notice Hebrews 9:14:

> "...how much more will the blood of Christ, who through the eternal Spirit offered Himself without blemish to God, cleanse your conscience from dead works to serve the living God?" *(NASB).*

The end result of *reality* is clearly seen in Galatians 5:22 and 23, which you can probably quote:

> "...the fruit of the Spirit is love, joy, peace, longsuffering, gentleness, goodness, faith, meekness, self-control" *(NASB).*

All right, let's zero in on this. The fruit of religion is the opposite of the fruit of the Holy Spirit. You show me someone who is religious, and I'll show you someone who doesn't have much joy. I'll show you someone who probably has hate. There is absolutely no one that can show more hatred than someone who is into religion, confronting someone who disagrees with them. Ever notice that? It's a negative, hateful spirit. They'll slash out and attack—rip apart. Joy? No, it's grrrrrrrrrrrr. You can sometimes irritate religious people just by smiling! It's as if it were a sin to be happy knowing Jesus.

And so, instead of peace, they have anxiety; instead of joy, they have sadness and despair; instead of love, hatred; they have patience with no one; they're incapable of gentleness when the chips are down—it's nothing but dead works. Which end result do you prefer?

Key Issue Number Six: the *Source*. The source of all religion is from the soulish, or fleshly realm; the source of *reality* is the Holy Spirit. Look at Hebrews 4:12:

> "...the word of God is living and active and sharper than any two-edged sword, and piercing as far as the division of soul and spirit, of both joints and marrow, and able to judge the thoughts and intentions of the heart" *(NASB)*.

So the Word of God, the Bible, is so sharp and so pointed that it can get clear down inside you. Some people speak out in tonuges and it's soulish. Some people worship and try to get it all built up but their heart's not in it—it's soulish worship. Some people witness ("I just gotta hand out tracts") it's a soulish thing. They're neglecting their family, their responsibilities—but someone told them they're supposed to be soul-winners. But is it the Holy Spirit leading them? If they hand out tracts out of guilt and a soulish motivation, the Holy Spirit has nothing to do with it; it's just religion. Anything you don't do by the leading of the Holy Spirit is religion! You may sit in church and sing, "Oh, how I love Jesus! Oh, how I love Jesus!"—and feel nothing from your heart. Oh, it's soulish! Do you understand Hebrews 4:12 now? The Word of God can separate the soul from the spirit—and do we ever need to get them separated! We need to distinguish between soulish motivation because someone makes us feel guilty—and the leadership of the Sovereign God.

Look at one of my favorite Scriptures, John 6:63:

> "It is the Spirit who gives life; the flesh profits nothing; the words that I have spoken to you are spirit and are life" *(NASB).*

Jesus was saying in effect, "Look, the flesh profits nothing." If you go out and witness to somebody, and God didn't tell you to go, it will profit nothing. That person won't be under conviction—in fact he might harden his heart against Jesus because you showed up and clobbered him and were obnoxious and rude. But when the Spirit's there, the witness brings life—it's quickened. Hallelujah!

I remember when somebody told me to go make a hospital call. I didn't believe the Lord wanted me to go at that time. So, I didn't want to go. ("I must go—it's my obligation—my duty. I'm a pastor; I'm supposed to be there, so here I go.") I didn't have on a black suit, but I might as well have . . . the religious role. ("Well, let me read a scripture before I go.") You know, it was dead—soulish. Two days later, the Holy Spirit spoke a verse to me in my private devotions for that same person. Man! Excited? I jumped in my car and tore off for the hospital. I said, "I have a word from the Lord for you: read this scripture." That person began to smile—it set him free. He was encouraged! That's the Spirit! He brings life! The source of religion is from your soul or your flesh; the source of *reality,* when God does something, is the Holy Ghost.

121

Now look at Key Issue Number Seven—*Attitude*. The attitude of the religious person is pharisaic, self-righteous, proud, judging; but the attitude of someone who is really in the presence of Jesus is patience and secret prayer. Look at the Scriptures carefully—Luke 18:9-14: "... He also told this parable to certain ones who trusted in themselves that they were righteous, and viewed others with contempt:" (in other words, with the nose elevated carefully one inch—now look at what he says) "Two men went up into the temple to pray." (Now they both went to church and they both went to pray—catch that? Two people walking into church together, both going to the temple, both to pray—one a Pharisee and the other a tax-collector. If you collect the taxes for a foreign empire, you're a Communist—a traitor. If the Russians took over and I collected taxes for the Russians, you wouldn't think much of me.) "The Pharisee stood and was praying thus to himself." (Notice—he and himself were having a good talk ... it doesn't say he was praying to God. *He* and *himself* were having a good talk. In other words, his prayer wasn't going any higher than his brain, nowhere near the throne of grace—and he was congratulating himself. Notice, he says:) "'God, I thank Thee that I'm not like other people, swindlers, unjust, adulterers, or even like this tax-gatherer. I fast twice a week;'" (Two times, God. Twice, God, You got that?) "'I pay tithes of all that I get.' But the tax-gatherer, standing some distance away, was even unwilling to lift his eyes to heaven," (he didn't figure he had any right to even look up) "but was beating his breast," (now notice next, the literal Greek translation used) "saying 'God, be merciful to me, the sinner!'" (not *a* sinner, but *the* sinner). "I tell you, this man went down to his house justified rather than the other; for everyone who exalts himself shall be humbled, but he who humbles himself shall be exalted" *(NASB)*. So if we begin to brag about how spiritual we are and how we're doing, God says, "I tell you, you're going to be humbled." The attitude of a religious person is to condemn everyone around them—to be self-righteous—("I don't do this; he does; I thank God I'm not like him.") This is dangerous.

Concerning the *reality* of secret prayer—why does Matthew 6:6 say to go in and shut the door? Is it just because God likes secret prayer? No, it's more essential and basic than that...it means you're telling it to *God alone.* Why shut the door if, when you come out, you tell everyone your prayer or what you're mad about? Your wife doesn't know about it if it's secret; your husband doesn't know your beefs. So often we leave the prayer closet and say, "Yeah, but God can't do it by Himself—I gotta tell!" We don't really believe in prayer.

A woman told me once, "My husband never corrects me—he just prays. And I'll tell my husband, 'You know, the Lord's been dealing with me about something.' And he'll say, 'Is that right?' and grin, and say, 'Well, praise the Lord!' And I'll find out later he's been praying about it." That's what it means to go into the closet and shut the door. It means we actually believe God can do it without our nagging. Nagging is the opposite of prayer; it's the position of someone who doesn't really believe God will actually come through. ("God can never show *my* husband anything; he's so blown-out, unspiritual, and wicked.") Well, that shows what you think of your prayer life, doesn't it? It shows that your righteousness is actually self-righteousness, and you don't really believe that God will hear your prayer. In that case, there's something basically wrong with your relationship with Jesus. When the relationship is right, the wife can pray things into her husband; a husband can pray things into his wife—without saying a word. Secret prayer and patience are the opposite of pride, self-righteousness, and judging. God has exposed self-righteousness and pride in me that was absolutely shocking. I never realized I was that way—the attitude of religion is to judge. "I thank God I'm not like that guy!"

Oh, children of the Most High God, let's be careful not to get self-righteous, proud, judgmental, and into religion. Do you see that nagging is the opposite of prayer? You children, if you see that you're dad is messed up, don't harp at him; get on your knees, shut the door, tell God, and never say one word to your dad, or to Mother, or whoever it may be. Then you have a secret—you and God have a secret together. You know what you've shared with God, and you can watch Him begin to answer, and you can then rejoice, having a secret praise-time with Him over it. And since you didn't have to nag or say a word; you know *you* had nothing to do with the improvement. God heard your prayer, and God answered from heaven. That's the opposite of religion.

We all have a lot of religion and self-righteousness in us—you might be thinking, "I'm glad I'm not like those religionists—particularly the (Baptists, or Lutherans, or Presbyterians, or whatever fits for you _____). I'm into Jesus and I'm not like that. Careful!

Key Issue Number Eight: the *Future Slant*. Religion institutionalizes the past, but we have glorious liberty in the reality of Jesus Christ. With religion, if you ever get a blessing, you institutionalize it—that's the origin of liturgy. Example: somebody wrote a good prayer, and it was so beautiful they just had to write it up and have everyone read it for the next twenty-two centuries. "Oh, Thou most omnipotent God." (Then the congregation responds:) "Oh, Thou most omnipotent God."

The same brother that wrote from jail about "organized crime and organized religion" also said that handing out bulletins before church is like going to one of

Shakespeare's plays: you're given a program telling you "what" is going to happen "when," and you *know* that there will be no deviation from it. The Holy Ghost couldn't move if He wanted to! It's all typed out—what He's going to do and when. There's even a little star on the side of the bulletin, telling you when to stand—you can't even sit down or stand up spontaneously! This indicates a future anticipation or "slant" of "doing it the way we've always done it." The status quo is good enough so keep it cool. Don't rock the boat; keep the peace—God won't do anything new! He finished it with the writing of Scripture! And when He *does* break through the religious facade to bless us, we set it up the same way and do the very same thing the next eighteen Sundays, hoping He'll do it again!

Key Issue Number Nine: *Focus*—the focus of religion is "do's" and "don'ts;" the focus of *reality,* is a love for Jesus Christ as Lord. Look at 1 Peter 3:3-4:

> "Whose adorning, let it not be that outward adorning of plaiting the hair, and of wearing of gold, or of putting on of apparel; But let it be the hidden man of the heart, in that which is not corruptible, even the ornament of a meek and quiet spirit, which is in the sight of God of great price."

It says here "no wearing of gold." It also says "no putting on of apparel." Anyone want to try *that* literally next Sunday? You'll find out about "church discipline" if you do! He's not saying here that you can't have a gold watch, or a dress; just not to let your adornment or attraction be that. He's not saying you have to look like an old "scrouth," like you haven't combed your hair in three weeks or washed it in three months. I've seen people who thought they were real saints who looked like that! First thing they do if they're a woman is tie their hair in a big knot and call it "holiness." ("No way you can call *my knot* plaiting.")

There are other groups that have a lot of rules about

hair, but it's all right to spend twenty-five dollars for a hairdo. Look out, though, if you spend a dollar and a half for some cheap earrings—then you're really into sin! Let's dig the meaning out of this passage: don't let the external things like hair and clothes and jewelry be your attraction, but a meek and quiet spirit which is precious to God. Some people follow those kinds of rules without the meek and quiet spirit—some, in fact, with a condemning, negative spirit, or whatever's the opposite of meek and quiet. The focus of *reality* with Jesus is this: "Thou shalt love the Lord thy God with all thy heart, mind, soul and strength." In other words, you fall in love with Jesus— you love Him so much that your "do's" and "don'ts" fall into place.

When my wife and I first met (don't tell anybody!), we danced! We never actually made a decision to quit dancing—we just got on fire for the Lord, and never did have any time for dancing. We just fell in love with Jesus and those things just dropped away . . . they lost interest for us, because we had something better. The focus of religion, the focus of its preaching and teaching, is the "do's" and "don'ts." The focus of *reality,* however, is to fall in love with Jesus—then you quit doing the other things that are unnecessary because you've found something better!

Key Issue Number Ten: *God's View.* I tell you, God hates religion; it's an abomination to Him. Some things upset Him more than others. Notice *Degrees of Sin* under the *Illustration* column. You understand, of course, that Jesus' actions and reactions were those which pleased the Father? So, then, we know about the Father through the Son. Jesus' view of things is God the Father's view of things—and I want to tell you that Jesus Christ was known to get angry without sinning—"Be ye angry, and sin not." When they brought the woman taken in adultery to Him, He simply said, "Go, and sin no more." No anger is implied. But the thing that really aroused His anger was religion—you remember how He went into the Temple and saw them making money from the religious rites, and He took a rope and "flat cleaned house!" He tipped over their money-changing tables, saying, "You made My house a den of robbers and it's to be a house of prayer." Oh, did He hate it. Nothing upsets God more than religion. Listen to Him:

> "But woe to you, scribes and Pharisees, hypocrites, because you shut off the kingdom of heaven from men, for you do not enter in yourselves; nor do you allow those who are entering to go in. (Woe to you, scribes and Pharisees, hypocrites, because you devour widows' houses, even while for a pretense you make long prayers; therefore you shall receive greater condemnation.)
>
> Woe to you, scribes and Pharisees, hypocrites, because you travel about on sea and land to make one proselyte; and when he becomes one, you make him twice as much a son of hell as yourselves. Woe to you, scribes and Pharisees, hypocrites! For you clean the outside of the cup and of the dish, but inside they are full of robbery and self-indulgence" (Matthew 23:13-15,25 *NASB*)

Oh, I tell you, when you get into religion, you and God are not going to be getting along too well. He hates it.

In Isaiah 1, God says He hates our solemn assemblies. I always liked that verse. "Solemn assemblies"—everything in place—no smiles, please! After all, it's got to be a *solemn* assembly. He says, "I hate them." Jesus gives God's view of religion, again, in another verse of Matthew 23—He says you strain at gnats and swallow camels. Picture that literally in your mind: Take a little cup and put a screen over it. We wouldn't want a gnat in our cup! Be real careful for gnats. Okay, no gnats. Then he says you swallow—(gulp)—a whole camel! Can you imagine? Somebody had to laugh when Jesus said that—I know I would have. You strain out insignificant gnats, then you swallow the whole camel! And we still do it today—we pick at tiny things. Example? Someone has on lipstick. That's a gnat for sure. "See? She wears lipstick—how brazenly sinful!" And yet, the person who is judging has a nice red spot of bitterness on the heart, is unforgiving, unmerciful, and self-righteous, and not in the least concerned about it. I couldn't care less whether a woman wears rouge or not; I'm more concerned about the condition of her heart.

Key Issue Eleven: *Mental or Spritual Condition.* Hebrews 4 is the key here—the writer says "you didn't enter into rest because of your unbelief." He's not talking about salvation. It would be false teaching to say that Joshua and Caleb were the only ones that "went to heaven" of those wilderness people. However, many are saved who haven't entered into His rest; who haven't fully entered into the Promised Land. Moses didn't get to Canaan, but he got to heaven; I also believe Miriam died in the wilderness, but I'm sure she went to heaven. Hebrews 4:1:

> "Therefore, let us fear lest, while a promise remains of entering His rest, any one of you should seem to have come short of it" (NASB).

Now verse 3:

> "For we who have believed enter that rest..."

There's a real rest when you quit trying to do it. Now look at verse 9:

> "There remains therefore a Sabbath rest for the people of God."

By the way, for anyone who puts unnecessary emphasis on the Sabbath, this is the only time in the Greek that this word is used in the New Testament. It says there remains a Sabbath rest. It doesn't show up that way in the King James translation, but it's the only time it's used in the New Testament...and the point of Hebrews 4 is the fulfillment of the Old Testament shadow of the Sabbath. It's the *rest of the Lord* that we're in *constantly*. The Old Testament says, "Don't commit adultery." God says in the New Testament, "Don't even lust." The Old Testament says to keep the Sabbath Day; God says in Hebrews 4 to get into a Sabbath rest twenty-four hours a day, every day.

Verse 10:

> "For the one who has entered His rest has himself also rested from his works, as God did from His."

So what does the word "rest" mean? Spiritually speaking, you quit working; a ceasing of labor. Start *believing* instead of working. We need to understand God's rest now, instead of five years from now. It'll save the Church a lot of trouble. *We* can't live the Christian life—never have been able to, never will be able to. The only One Who can live it is Jesus, and we must let Him live it through us instead of striving and straining and working. We must all start *believing*.

Look at verse 3 again: "We who have *believed*..." "I believe You, Jesus, to be meek through me; I believe You, Jesus, to be pure through me." Everything we need was finished from the foundation of the world—even the works we can't do in ourselves. All we need to do is believe it! The end of verse 3 says, "... His works were finished from the foundation of the world."

I'm still rejoicing over the time recently when I had sinned and I felt the need of lengthy repentance. I thought, "I've gotta get down and repent and get this out of me." Suddenly Jesus said, "If you confess it as sin and believe you're dead to it, you are." I hadn't even had time to get to my knees when He said it. So I just replied, *"I believe it, Lord,"* and I haven't been tempted since. You wonder if it could be that simple? It won't be, if we try to get our own victory. We could work and strive for ten years and still come up short. But if we say, "Lord, You say I'm dead to it, so I believe it, hallelujah. My old nature was crucified with Christ on the cross. It's true; it's Your Word; I believe it." It's by faith that we enter into rest, ceasing from our own works. We can then say, "Lord, love through me, be sweet through me. Here I am, Lord; just live Your life through me." We can lean back in His arms and let Him do it; it takes all the pressure off. If we can grasp this, we've entered into the opposite of religion.

Religion brings guilt and anxiety, turmoil and unhappiness. *You'll never find a happy legalist,* because of the misery of always failing to keep the rules; always being in bondage. It's impossible to be a legalist and be happy.

Key Issue Number Twelve is the *Method of Salvation.* Now we're down to the nitty-gritty, and this is the basic issue—whether we're going to be saved by our works and the keeping of the law, or whether we'll be saved through faith and by the grace of God.

> "For by grace you have been saved through faith; and that not of yourselves, it is the gift of God; not as a result of works, that no one should boast" (Ephesians 2:8-9 *NASB).*

I want you to know that there's a spirit of false repentance. It's very much like the conviction of the Holy Spirit—it's so close. It's subtle and tricky, but it's a *wrong spirit.* It sounds like repentance, but it has hatred and condemnation with it. Where it seems to produce obedience, instead, it produces works. Where it is being manifested, people talk like this:

> "Bless God, all these other churches aren't sincere! *We* believe in keeping the whole Bible! If you're not keeping it *all,* brother, you're not going to make it! You've got to keep every verse of it ... *everything!* If you don't, you're not going to make it to heaven! The people over in so-and-so's church smoke, drink,—and the way they carry on! They're not going to make it!"

And, if we don't watch it, something inside of us will respond to that. And we'll say, "That's just what I believe—I believe in holiness," but there's just a little check in our spirits, because we realize the spirit of that statement is wrong.

Notice the spirit of their convictions includes phrases like "we must" and "we've got to" and "we've got to keep." And notice the hatred. Although you believe in holiness, purity, and chastity, yet somehow the spirit of the thing is negative, hateful, critical and judgmental—in short, pharisaic. It sounds like they're really repenting, but they're not resting! I talked to a brother on the phone, and he said, "We believe in this." I replied, "Well, I do, too." He said, "We believe in that." I answered, "I do, too." He continued, "We believe in that." I said, "So do I." You know, I began to go along with him until I noticed a change in his emphasis. He began to say, "We've got to...we've got to endure...we've got to keep...we must do all the Scriptures..." It sounded good, but his faith was in his ability to do it, rather than in Jesus Christ. I plan to keep every verse in the Bible, but I know it will be through Jesus Christ living through me, and not my doing it.

One way to spot a pharisaic and critical spirit of false repentance is the lack of joy with it; there's no peace with it; there's no love with it. Its fruit is bad; if there's no joy with it, it's faulty.

I can remember a happy repentance—it was a time of joy. I believe repentance should result in shouting for joy after the sorrow. Now if the fruit of the Holy Spirit isn't there, the spirit of the thing is wrong, even if the words are there. I exhort you to beware of those who get you back to dead works and out of the rest of the Lord.

In summary, we know that when we hear religion being preached, it's bad news; it's rules; it's bondage. But we should want to kiss the feet of the one who brings good news—the news that we can really be happy; that it's Christ instead of laws; that it's personal presence and a personal relationship with Jesus, instead of a lot of rules and bondage. That *Jesus Christ* is the Lord that reigns!

Has this chapter helped you? It nails some things down for me. In the future, when you're asked to explain the difference between religion and a relationship with Jesus, you have it listed here for you—source, attitude, motivation, who's Lord, the mental condition of both types, the method of salvation of both types—the whole ballgame.

So remember that Satan loves "religion" . . . he's busy in the "church-building, rule-setting business;" his subtle attack is from the rear. Don't let religious spirits cheat you out of a real walk with Jesus by condemning you with Leviticus 28. When you think you've successfully condensed the Christian walk to a formula of rules, you're out of *reality* and into religion—out of the joy of praying and seeking the beauty of His presence, and into the drudgery and trickery of empty rules.

I know the Lord gave me the material for this chapter; I needed it personally, and I know the Body of Christ needs it. The significance of this chapter may be too deep for you to grasp totally. None of us have understood it as deeply as we need to understand. I feel this is a key concept because it shakes the whole attitude of approach to the ministry.

CHAPTER

7

Testing the Spirits

"Beloved, believe not every spirit, but *try the spirits* whether they are of God: because many false prophets are gone out into the world. Hereby know ye the Spirit of God: Every spirit that confesseth that Jesus Christ is come in the flesh is of God:

And every spirit that confesseth not that Jesus Christ is come in the flesh is not of God: and this is that spirit of antichrist, whereof ye have heard that it should come; and even now already is it in the world" (1 John 4:1-3).

The **first test** John gives is to discern whether the spirit speaking out of a person will confess that Jesus Christ is the Messiah; that Jesus is really God in human flesh. (Every time a person speaks, you hear a spirit speaking: the human spirit, the Holy Spirit, or a spirit of the antichrist.)

"...who desires all men to be saved and to come to the knowledge of the truth. For there is one God, and one mediator also between God and men, the man Christ Jesus, who gave Himself as a ransom for all, the testimony borne at the proper time" (1 Timothy 2:4-6 *NASB*).

God says He wants everyone to be saved, to come to the knowledge of the truth. I taught one afternoon in one of the high schools of the city—a philosophy class. I've been there four times; the teacher invites me every semester. This particular time I was denouncing the occult, and one of the girls raised her hand and said, "Why do you put down eastern religions?" God helped me with my answer—I said, "Well, Jesus said that He was the door, and if anyone climbed up any other way he was a thief and a robber. If you try to climb up through the occult and eastern religions, you'll find they're demonism: they're thieves and robbers. They'll rob you of your soul, steal your peace, your joy, your happiness, and you'll end up in occult oppression and bondage."

She said, "Well, I believe some of what Jesus said, but I believe that He's just *one* way."

I said, "You're saying that Jesus Christ is a liar, because He said 'I am *the* way, and *the* truth, and *the* life, and no man comes to the Father *but by me*,' and either Jesus Christ is a liar and a false prophet or He's the Son of God, and you've got to get off the fence!"

She quipped, "You're awfully biased."

And I answered, "I admit I am biased, but I want to be dogmatically sweet."

At that, the whole class laughed, and she could sense the sweetness of my reply—my spirit—and I know that God really got through to her. One of the "Jesus kids" there, a real Christian, told me after the class, "That girl that was raising all those questions isn't a believer yet."

You see, there's only "one mediator between God and men, the *man* Christ Jesus" (1 Timothy 2:5). Notice it doesn't say the "Son of God, Christ Jesus" here. True, He *is* the Son of God, but the emphasis here is that Jesus had to literally become a man in order to become a mediator. So the inspired wording by the Holy Spirit reads "the *man* Christ Jesus." False teaching denies the *deity* of Jesus, or denies the *humanity* of Jesus. Either teaching is false. For Him to be mediator, He had to be a man and overcome sin as a man; to be mediator, He also had to be God. To represent God He had to be God; to represent men He had to be man—Jesus Christ had to be God-man, but whenever Scripture describes Him as mediator, it always emphasizes the fact that He was a man. He didn't live the Christian life as God, because He was man. He said, "I can do nothing without the Father." He lived in total submission to God in the power of the Holy Spirit, and He didn't use any supernatural power to overcome sin that we as Christians don't have! He proved it could be done; He did it. Any spirit that denies this teaching is antichrist.

> "We are of God: he that knoweth God heareth us; he that is not of God heareth not us. Hereby know we the spirit of truth, and the spirit of error" (1 John 4:6).

John says, "if they hear us"— who does he mean by "us?" He means all those who have written God's Word— the Scriptures. This is the **second test.** Everyone who is of God will agree with what Paul said, or what Jude, James, Luke, or Matthew said. Suppose I'm teaching on hell: someone says, "I know that's in the Bible, *but* I don't believe it." That person manifests that they're not of the Holy Spirit. They're of a different spirit if they don't hear what the Scriptures say. Do you consider yourself wiser than the apostles? Who are you? It's the height of pride to disagree with the Word of God. You have made yourself your own authority, when the only real authority is the Bible.

One of the basic questions of life, is, "What is my authority?" We can say, "Well, so-and-so thinks this, so-and-so thinks that; this pastor thinks this, that preacher says that." It doesn't make a bit of difference what you or I think or say; your idea about religion is as good as mine. What we all need to do is find out what God's idea is—in His Word. If it's in the Bible, it's true; if your premise disagrees with Scripture, it's error. Readjust your theology until it agrees with the Bible instead of readjusting the Bible until it agrees with your theology.

By disagreeing with Scripture, we make our little pea-brain an idol. We say, "I don't understand that; it doesn't seem reasonable to me; therefore it couldn't be true." We've made an authority—an idol—of our brain and our understanding. *The Word of God is true.* Jesus said, "Thy Scripture is true—Thy Word is true." If you disagree with Scripture, you're not of God.

What if John could come back, stand in your church and say: "We are of God; he who knows God hears us and he that is not of God hears not us." Would you think John full of presumption and pride? If so, you have the wrong spirit. If we're of God, we'll agree with John and the other apostles; if 1 John 4:6 irritates you, you have a wrong spirit.

Everyone has to have authority underlying his actions and statements. When Jesus cleansed the temple He was asked "By what authority do you do this?" If I tell you that I believe a certain fact, you have the right to question the authority for my belief. If, furthermore, you don't accept the Bible as my authority and you say, "to you the Bible is a paper pope," then I plead guilty. As far as I'm concerned, the Scripture is infallible, and whatever it says is the basis for the direction of my life. If the Bible isn't your authority, then your brain may be, or your denominational background. A lady once told me, "I know the baptism in the Holy Spirit is taught in the Scriptures, but we don't believe it; therefore it's not true." What she was really saying was that *her church is her authority instead of Scripture.*

Something unusual happened to one of the ladies in our church—we'll call her Mrs. Jones. The Lord spoke to her and said, "How would your husband like it if he came home one night and you said, 'I've decided to go by the name of Mrs. Smith?' (Can you imagine what you men would say to that?) I know what I'd tell my wife, Dee:

"You're *my* wife, and you're taking *my* name and no other!" The Lord told her, "Take no other name but the name of Jesus—you're My bride and you're to take no other name but Mine. You're not to take the name of John the Baptist, Martin Luther, Pentecostal, Charismatic—no other name but the name of Jesus." That was definitely a word from the Lord!

What denomination are you? A brother in Holland shared this with me: "When people ask what church I'm from, if I say a charismatic church, or a pentecostal church, or a holiness church, or what-have-you church, then they're free to say, 'Oh, yes . . . well, we don't believe in that'—and they're off the hook! I like to play with them a little, so I just say, 'We just love the Word of God.' They usually persist, with 'Well, what label is it?' I then say, 'Different people call us different names, but let me show you this verse of Scripture,' and I get them into the Word of God. I never tell them what we are, and that way they have to stay in the Word." That's really the wisdom of God, because as soon as you say, "We're full-gospel" (or whatever), they say, "Oh!" and with one shrug of the shoulders they're out from under conviction. Isn't that wisdom?

> "Beloved, let us love one another: for love is of God; and every one that loveth is born of God, and knoweth God. He that loveth not knoweth not God; for God is love (1 John 4:7-8).

The **third test** of the spirits is to determine whether God's love is present. Don't try to explain away this Scripture; it's true. I once had a vision while preaching. Just as the sharp, two-edged sword, the Word of God, was going forth—just ready to cut and get people under the conviction of the Holy Spirit, a saw appeared, sawing off the point of that sword, sawing off all the edges so it wouldn't really cut anyone, just as God was ready and willing to deliver them from hypocrisy and religion and show them they were not really saved yet. How does this happen? We read the Word and send it forth, then get out in front of the Sword and say, "Well, it doesn't really mean that." Many people read 1 John 4:7-8 and say, "Well, I know a lot of people who don't show love, and I know they're saved, so that verse doesn't really mean that." What they're really saying is, "That Scripture doesn't apply to me." "He that loves not, knows not God, for God is love." That's the Word of God, so let's leave it sharp; don't blunt it or take anything off it! A person may be a fundamentalist and believe all the doctrines of the Bible, but if they don't have love, they don't know God. If a "full-gospel Christian" is sarcastic and hateful and fighting, the love of God isn't in that person.

Consider this scripture verse just as it is and examine your reaction: perhaps you're thinking "I've gone to church all my life, but I certainly don't have love." That's good for you to admit if it's true—perhaps the Holy Spirit is trying to show you that you're not really saved yet. Or, perhaps you have another reaction: "Of course that's what the Scriptures say—I believe it's true but it's not for me . . . I don't accept it." (That's billy goat religion—"yes, but"—"but, but.") We can believe the Scriptures in our head, but not let them penetrate our heart. Respond to the message, and fall into the right category, saying, "I believe all of Scripture; I repent; I shall get real; I shall get this love." Many people avoid the cutting edge of this verse and put a mental replacement there—example: "Beloved, let us not smoke." I don't believe in smoking, but I've seen people who smoke who have more love than some, like the Pharisees, who "don't smoke!" Let's get first things first: it's love that is *most important*.

You may know *about* God without *knowing* God— know all the correct doctrines without knowing Him yet.

You may know that Jesus was born in Bethlehem, raised in Nazareth as a carpenter, baptized in the Jordan River by John the Baptist, crucified for your sins, rose again the third day, ascended back to heaven—but still not know God. I know the President of the United States—that is, I know a lot about his background, his family, but I've never sat down with him or talked to him. I don't have a personal relationship with him.

It's the same way with Jesus—you may know about Him, but did you ever sit down and talk with Him? Is He real to you? Is He inside of you? Do you know Him? When you get the Spirit of God inside you, the Spirit of God is the Spirit of love, and love will be manifest in you. If you don't "have the goods," you don't have the Savior, and the "goods" of 1 John 4 is love.

This is what the Lord is saying: "Thou shalt love thy neighbor into salvation, and thou shalt love thy husband into salvation, for surely it is the flow of the Spirit that brings people to Me, and My Spirit is a manifestation of love. Therefore, be a sweet one and be thou a lover of all men, and thou shalt see people won to Me."

I know a girl that left home, went into dope and rebellion, and then found Jesus. As soon as she was saved, she went home, approached her Dad and asked, "Are you saved?" Of course, he really got hot about it, and her witness was not accepted. She soon realized that the Lord wanted her to move back home, submit to her parents, and let her *life* show the family God's love and power. She told me the Lord wouldn't let her "witness" in the usual sense, but she tells it like this: "All I did was just smile. I'd come in and say, 'Hi, Daddy!' and I'd kiss him on the cheek." Guess what? On a recent Sunday her father said, "We're all going to church." Does he ever love and appreciate his daughter now! He'd fight to uphold her honor.

As I was talking with her, the Lord showed me

something. His word of wisdom was "You are the salt of the earth—and salt comes in grains." When she kissed her daddy on the cheek, that was just one grain of salt. It takes less than a teaspoon for the potatoes. Some of you put a cupful of salt in Hubby's oatmeal every morning. "When are you going to church? When are you going to be the spiritual head of the family? You know what the Bible says you ought to do!" You're too salty! When you put a tablespoonful in the potatoes, nobody can eat it! God hasn't called you sisters to be a personal preacher to your husbands! As long as you continue your preaching, he isn't going to get saved! You're not his high priest, ordained of God to preach him a sermon three times a week! Just be kind; be sweet; just be a grain of salt here; a grain there.

By contrast, people can't resist love; everyone is crying out for it. Little babies, little children, teenagers, middle-aged people, old people—everyone wants to be loved. And few can resist love when it's the love of God. It isn't your doctrine or your words that move people; it's your heart attitude of love. Let's test our own spirits, not just someone else's spirit. I'm afraid for people who're *dead sure* they're right, but they're full of hatred.

> "In this was manifested the love of God toward us, because that God sent his only begotten Son into the world, that we might live through him" (1 John 4:9).

The **fourth test** is the "blood test." They must accept the blood atonement of Jesus! Hallelujah for the blood!

> "The blood of Jesus Christ, His Son, cleanses us from all sin" (1 John 1:7 *NASB*).

The blood of Jesus Christ can cleanse away depression, cleanse away fear—cleanse from all sin. People ask me, "How can I get rid of my unbelief?" I don't know of any way other than through the blood of Jesus . . . just treat it like any other sin, praying, "God, I'm guilty of unbelief—I call it what it is. Wash it out of me with your blood, in Jesus' name," and that will get rid of the unbelief. If we believe in the blood of Jesus, we can get instant deliverance from any demon. If I feel like I've got something contrary to the life of Jesus in my life, I kneel down and ask the blood to cleanse it out of me. Then I get up, I believe it's gone, and go about my work. I don't spend a lot of time worrying about it.

Recently I was approached by a young man wanting deliverance. I spent thirty minutes trying to teach him to just believe "Brother, just let it go!" I thought he was going to wear himself out—I think, in fact, that he did just that. Deliverance is by *faith* in the blood of Jesus, not anything else. If you believe you're free, you are! If you don't believe you're free, you aren't!

The Lord keeps showing me things about deliverance, for example, this verse of Scripture:

> "If any one supposes that he knows anything, he has not yet known as he ought to know" (1 Corinthians 8:2 *NASB*).

Sometimes I'll approach a deliverance situation determined that I'm not even going to pray with that person initially—I'm just going to show them their deliverance in the Word of God and make them believe it—and the Lord will tell me to pray with them, and cast it out of them. The next time, I say, "I'm going to run that devil out!"—and the Lord won't even let me pray with them! He tells me to show them the Word. I get so tickled—just when I think I have it figured out, God switches, *every time*. So I just don't know anything—I really don't! (That's not humility, it's just a fact.) And I can tell when I'm moving out of the Spirit: I'm headed in a certain direction and I don't feel any anointing on it—I just feel "blah!" What happened? I slipped out of the stream. The Spirit was going one way and I was going the other; the stream wiggled and I didn't wiggle with the stream. Have you ever seen the Jordan River? From the sky, it looks like a snake. The Holy Spirit is the river of life; we've got to move with the river, or we'll end up stuck in the sand!

Let's return to 1 John 4:9 on love—"In this was manifested..." The word translated here "manifested" means "clearly demonstrated." What was clearly demonstrated? The verse continues: "the love of God toward us." How was it demonstrated? "God sent his only begotten Son into the world." Why did He send Jesus—just so we might not have to go to hell? Let's finish the verse: "...that we might *live* through him." If I had to tell you that Jesus Christ came from heaven to die on a cross to save you from hell, but before you make it to heaven you have to go on lusting and hating and being jealous and depressed, I'd be ashamed to preach it! No! He died on a cross that we might live! Look at 2 Corinthians 4:10:

> "Always bearing about in the body the dying of the Lord Jesus, that the life also of Jesus might be made manifest in our body."

Jesus is looking for bodies in which He can manifest His life. He wants every one of you to be like Him in your home, in your situation. He wants you to be a manifestation of Him. Think of it: when you walk into a room, it should be just like Jesus walking into that room.

Notice the ending of the verse: "...that the life also of Jesus might be made manifest..." —manifest *where?* "....*in our body.*" It doesn't say our "glorified body." It's not in the "sweet bye and bye." It's in the mortal flesh, here and now. Paul continues:

> "For we which live are always delivered unto death for Jesus' sake, that the life also of Jesus might be made manifest in our mortal flesh" (2 Corinthians 4:11).

What does it mean, "always bearing about in the body the dying of the Lord Jesus?" What does it mean, "always delivered unto death for Jesus' sake?" Jesus said we should deny self, take up the cross daily, and follow Him. Paul is saying the same thing. Example: if someone says something to hurt you, you reckon yourself dead to it and keep your mouth shut. If your husband crosses you, instead of answering back you die to that desire, bearing about in your body the dying of the Lord Jesus. You reckon yourself dead to revenge, dead to hatred. Here comes a thought of lust: you're dead to that—you take up your cross, saying, "I used to live that way, but I don't live that way anymore." Here comes a thought to get jealous and envious! You immediately respond: "I'm dead to that!" You constantly reckon yourself dead to everything that's not like Jesus, and then the life of Jesus can come forth in your life.

Notice the little word "always" in verse 10—not just when the going is smooth... "*always* bearing about in the body the dying..." Also notice in verse 11 that we do it "for Jesus' sake." We don't do it for our spouse's sake or for our neighbor's sake, but for Jesus' sake. We forgive them for Jesus' sake; we keep our mouth shut for Jesus' sake.

Now we continue to verse 12:

"So then death worketh in us, but life in you."

If we can stand up at the end of the day and say, "death worked in me, but life worked in you," then, hallelujah, we've been in the Spirit! Let's say we had four little trials today. One trial was to get mad at somebody, another was to be impatient, another was to tell somebody off, and another little trial was the temptation to shoplift. I'm convinced that stealing is one of the main temptations of the 20th century. If we reckoned ourselves dead to all those things, then we can say, "Death worked in me but life worked in all those of my family." But—if we blew our cool and death didn't work in us, then we let our old nature live, and death worked in those around us, as we wounded and hurt them. "Death works in us, but *life* in you." Here—Now—Today. Remember what John said in 1 John 4:9? "...that we might *live* through him." This life of Christ is not just for the next world, it's for this world. Hallelujah!

> "Herein is love, not that we loved God, but that he loved us, and sent his Son to be the propitiation for our sins...We love him, because he first loved us" (1 John 4:10,19).

Do you know how Jesus Christ conquers us? Through His love. I remember as a new Christian, when I first discovered that Jesus would keep me, I just wept before the Lord. I found out that He loved me so much He not only died for me, but would forgive me when I sinned. I didn't say, "Yippee! I can go sin! Jesus will forgive me!" Instead, I said, "Jesus, I don't want to hurt You. If You love me that much, how can I let You down?" When I saw that He loved me so much, it produced more love for Him in me. In the Greek, the verb used here is the strongest possible verb. The literal Greek translates this way: "Herein is love, not that we *have* loved Him or that we *presently* love Him, but that He loves us."

Let's apply this principle to husbands. You brothers will never preach your wives into submission; instead, you love her into submission. You parents, I know there's a place for the rod, but you can love children into submission. It's love that makes people want to be submissive. Love begets love.

If you're having trouble with a certain sin in your life, I suggest praying this way: "Jesus, show me how much You love me," because if you fall in love with Jesus, you'll fall out of love with sin. It's love for Jesus that produces victory. Paul is praying this way in Ephesians 3:19— "...to know the love of Christ which passeth knowledge..." And what is the result of knowing this love? "...that ye might be filled with all the fulness of God." I noticed one day, as I was reading through the

Gospels, that I could read about the crucifixion as though it were merely a factual account. I began to pray that the Lord would really show me the cross—to see Him hanging there. When you see Jesus' suffering on the cross and know that it wasn't just because of Pilate or Judas, but because He loved *you* and because He was thinking about *you* that put Him there, you'll be filled with the fulness of God. The more you see how much Jesus loves you, the more you'll love Him, and the more you'll be filled with all the fullness of God. I pray the Lord will show you this by revelation. Ask the Holy Spirit to make it new to you. God loved you so much, He sent His Son to be a propitiation for your sin. "Propitiation" means "a sacrifice to avert wrath." If Jesus hadn't shed His blood and been damned in your place, the only thing that you would have to look forward to is wrath—the wrath of God and the lake of fire.

As a pastor, I can preach against sin and it won't produce much holiness. But if I stand and preach a message of Jesus—a whole sermon about nothing but Jesus, until people really get a glimpse of the Lord, they'll leave the church determined never to sin. It isn't only preaching against sin that produces holiness (although we should take a stand against sin); it's the *lifting up of Jesus* that produces holiness. When you see how much Jesus loves you, then you're not going to want to hurt Him. So instead of lifting up sin, lifting up repentance (as important as it is), we need to lift up Jesus Christ. Anyone who gets a revelation of Jesus hanging on the cross for their sin (not in the head but in the heart) will repent. So, let's talk about Jesus.

"Beloved, if God so loved us, we ought also to love one another. No man hath seen God at any time. If we love one another, God dwelleth in us, and his love is perfected in us" (1 John 4:11-12).

Now, why does he say, "No man hath seen God at any

145

time"—and stick it right in the middle of his talk about love? Nobody has ever seen God the Father, but if you have the love of Jesus in you, *then people will see God in you.* In John 14:9 Jesus says, "he that hath seen me hath seen the Father." So your husband should be able to say, "I've seen God—I've seen the love of Jesus in my wife." Remember my illustration of the girl and her daddy? He saw Jesus in her. What people need is not words about Jesus; they need to see Him in us. If they can see Him in us, they'll want Him. It's so sad when they look at us and they don't want what we have... if only they could look and say, "I wish I could be a woman like that—or a man like that."

"Hereby know we that we dwell in him, and he in us, because he hath given us of his Spirit" (1 John 4:13).

The **fifth test** of the spirits is the possession of the Holy Spirit. Now we're testing ourselves. Notice he says, "Hereby *know* we..." It's not doubt, it's not wish, not wonder, not hope, not "keep your fingers crossed," not "wait until you die and see Him"—but "Hereby *know* we" that we dwell in Jesus and Jesus in us—because Jesus has given us of His Spirit. We don't know that we dwell in Him because of religion. With religion: you join a church, shake a preacher's hand, get baptized, plunged, dipped, poured, immersed, and all that does for you is make you a wet sinner. You could be baptized by every preacher in America and still come up a wet sinner.

We already spoke of all the differences between having Jesus and having religion. Do you have the Holy Spirit? We know we dwell in Him because He's given us of His Spirit. Is the Spirit of God in you? I can remember the day and the hour when He came into me... I've got something inside me besides just me. Do you have something inside you besides just you? That's the best way I know to put salvation...you see, it's not a mind trick, it's not mental gymnastics. Christianity is not a philosophy—it's not rearranging your mind and saying, "I'll accept this precept or this concept." No, to get saved is to have the Holy Spirit (Who exists independently of you) come inside you and live. That's what it means to be born of the Spirit.

Many people go to church, but the Spirit never came into them. They have correct doctrine, but the Spirit isn't dwelling within. Religion is going through the church trips without the Spirit, and the devil loves it. He knows that all those poor people think they're going to go to heaven, when they're actually just "drugged" on religion. So they have a false security—a dangerous business. God gives us true security: "Hereby know we that we dwell in him, and he in us, because he hath given us of his Spirit." We shouldn't have to have a preacher tell us that we're saved. I prefer God to tell me that I'm saved! The Bible says, "The Spirit Himself bears witness with our spirit that we are children of God" (Romans 8:16, *NASB*). If you don't have the witness of the Holy Spirit that you're saved, I wouldn't take any chances! You can't afford to depend on some friend or a pastor to tell you you're saved. If you don't know what it is to have the Spirit in you, it's time, by the grace of God, that you find out. That doesn't necessarily mean you're a hypocrite; it may just mean you're strictly religious and sadly lost. *Do* you have His Spirit? Check with the Word of God and ask the Lord in prayer to show you what your place in Him is, that by His grace you might *know* that you are saved.

"And we have seen and do testify that the Father sent the Son to be the Savior of the world. Whosoever shall confess that Jesus is the Son of God, God dwelleth in him, and he in God" (1 John 4:14-15).

The **sixth test** of the spirits is confessing that Jesus is the Savior; the **seventh** is confessing that Jesus is the Son of God. If we confess that Jesus is the Son of God, then we can't disagree with Him. However, if we disagree with what Jesus says, and contradict what He says, we don't really believe that Jesus is the Son of God. Suppose I tell you that I believe Jesus is the Son of God. Then, as I read what He says in Scripture, I attempt to explain it away, saying, "Well, I don't really believe He meant that—I believe what I believe instead of what Jesus said"—what I'm really telling you by that is that I don't believe He's the Son of God! Once you confess that He's the Son of God, you've accepted the underlying authority of His words as being infallible, and everything He said is correct, absolutely true, and cannot be disputed. So you're forced to the ultimate question, "Who is Jesus Christ?" and, you're forced off the fence! He's either the Son of God, or He's the biggest lunatic, deceiver, and false prophet the world has ever seen!

Jesus stood up one day and looked over a crowd of people and He made some amazing statements. For example, He said, "I am the way, the truth and the life: no man cometh unto the Father, but by me" (John 14:6). Now think about that for a minute. What if *I* were to say, "*I* am the way, *I* am the truth, *I* am the life, and nobody goes to God the Father but by *me*?" What would you think about *me* if *I* said that? The Jewish people heard a man say that! They only had two choices: either He's a liar, a false prophet, a deceiver and a lunatic, or else He is Who He claims to be, the Son of God. And today, as well, there is no other choice. You can't say He's a good teacher and deny He is the Son of God; if He isn't the Son of God, He was a liar! A good teacher doesn't deceive people; a good teacher is not a liar. I can tell you *about* the way; Jesus said, "I *am* the way." I can tell you *about* the truth;

Jesus said, "I *am* the truth." I can tell you *about* the life; Jesus said, "I *am* the life." We must either say, "That's correct; that's true; He is God the Son," or else we must say, "He was a false teacher, a deceiver, and a lunatic." The Scriptures say, in effect, that when someone says, with full understanding, "I know—I believe—that Jesus is the Son of God," then God dwells in that person, and he in God. But if someone denies the deity of Jesus, then they're not born again...they're not saved.

Jesus told us what the foundation of the church was. One day He pinned His disciples down on this question, just as He's pinning us down right now, saying, "Whom do men say that I am?" (Mark 8:27, Matthew 16:13). And they answered Him, "Some say John the Baptist; some, Elijah; and others, Jeremiah, or one of the prophets." (In other words, "Some say you're a good teacher, and a prophet, and a mighty man of God.") But Jesus wasn't satisfied with that. He said, "But who do *you* say that I am?" Peter answered, "Thou art the Christ (literally, "the Messiah"), the Son of the living God." When Peter said that, Jesus looked Peter in the eye and He said, "Upon this rock" (*what* rock?—the confession that Jesus is the Messiah, the Son of God)—"Upon this rock the church is built." If you deny that Jesus is the Messiah, the Son of the Living God, you're not on the rock, you're on another foundation. You're on shifting sand. The wind and the waves and the storm are already blowing across this world, and your house is going to sink—because you're not saved yet! The foundation of the church is the rock of Peter's confession. Peter didn't just get that confession in his head; it came by revelation. Jesus said, "...flesh and blood did not reveal this to you, but My Father who is in heaven." So Peter got a revelation from God—it was no "head trip."

Let's look at it again (Matthew 16:18): "...thou art

Peter, and upon this rock..." What rock? He actually says in the Greek, "Thou art *Petros* (masculine gender), but upon this *petra* (feminine gender) is the church built." So, He switched Greek words, He switched genders. There's no way that rock could be a person, or *Petros*. The "rock" upon which the church is built is the confession, "Thou art the Christ, the Son of the living God." I announce to you that I know that Jesus is the Messiah, the Son of the Living God. Because I believe this, I'm on the rock, my feet are firmly settled, and I'm not going to be blown over. And that must be your confession, if it isn't then you don't really know Jesus yet—even if you're a church member and you're religious. If you don't accept Jesus, on Judgment Day you'll hear these words played back to you, and you'll be without excuse—these words are truth. Again, "Whosoever shall confess that Jesus is the Son of God, God dwelleth in him, and he in God."

"But when He, the Spirit of truth comes, He will guide you into all the truth..." (John 16:13a *NASB*).

The **eighth test** of what spirit is manifested and probably the most important, is best illustrated by an experience which I had that I would like to relate here. The circumstances are altered to respect the people involved. I was asked to perform a wedding some time ago, and everything in preparation had gone well until the "big day." I believe in taking every opportunity to share the reality of Jesus, whether it's a counseling session, a worship service, or conducting a formal ceremony as in a wedding or funeral—*as the Spirit leads*. Before this particular ceremony, my wife, Dee, was praying for me as follows: "Lord, guide Ernie today in the discerning of spirits."

When we arrived at the church, the atmosphere was cold—something was very wrong. It seems that the families involved had had a serious disagreement the previous night, and some of them had nearly come to blows over their disagreement, which centered around the bride and groom. There was even talk of calling off the wedding, and some of the women in the wedding party were in tears. This was a very disheartening situation, and there was tension in every face. I wondered whether I should go ahead with what I believed the Lord had told me, to share a salvation message during the ceremony, or to share a message on love—it seemed that these people needed to be ministered to concerning love. As I was praying in the Spirit and seeking the Lord for direction, He spoke to me and gave me peace about preaching on salvation, just as He'd told me earlier. A wedding ceremony should be more than just words and empty phrases—and I wanted to be obedient to the Holy Spirit.

You know, as I began to share a straightforward message of Jesus, I found that I was under a heavy anointing of the Spirit. The message was so sweet—so gentle—so full of Jesus' love, that I could see the tension and the worry and the fear and the mistrust leave those faces. You could see a physical change in those people. And, it was so easy! I was almost a spectator—watching the Holy Spirit minister through that message—I didn't have to work at fighting those contrary spirits. At the end of the ceremony I was relieved to see that we'd "made it." (Some had threatened that there would be physical violence before they'd let those two young people get married.)

Afterwards, during the reception, the tension was building again, and a spiritual, dark cloud seemed to descend on the group. Again, I inwardly sought the direction of the Lord, and I immediately felt led to finish off the reception with prayer. When the time was right, I asked for silence and began to pray. It was like a benediction—both on the newlyweds and the friends and families gathered. I ended the prayer something like this: "...and Lord, I just declare Your peace on this couple and all these people here—Your peace, Lord, in Jesus' name. Amen." During the first few moments of silence following the prayer, one hesitant, but rather loud, sarcastic voice was heard to say, *"Well, there isn't any peace here!"* It was like a shockwave to my heart. I wondered what was going to happen next—and then someone giggled. Someone else gave a nervous little laugh. Then one brave soul just guffawed, and soon everyone was laughing! The tension was broken! Suddenly I realized, "The power of the enemy is broken! The peace of the Lord is here! The spirits who came to disrupt—to begin this marriage in discord—to foment jealousy, hatred, and bitterness—they're defeated in Jesus' name!" So I just praised the Lord amid the hilarity.

Later, the Lord showed me something in retrospect. I remembered my wife's prayer: "Lord, guide Ernie today in the discerning of spirits." In that moment, I knew that He had done much more than that. I probably couldn't have named all the messengers of Satan sent to steal happiness that day, but the Lord spoke to me and said, "It was the voice of My Spirit you discerned this day. When you obeyed *Me,* preaching on salvation, My anointing was on that place. When you heard and obeyed *Me,* praying for My peace, My anointing was there. The Spirit you need most to discern is *MY SPIRIT.*"

Hallelujah! Jesus told us that when He, the Spirit of truth comes, *He will guide us into all the truth.* His direction is available as we seek Him, in obedience to Him and having repented from known sin. Many spirits are speaking words of deceit and religion today; I want to hear words of truth and reality from the Holy Spirit. The Holy Spirit came on the day of Pentecost, and His guidance has been available ever since. When we learn to discern the voice of the *Holy* Spirit, we'll have no need to discern the *other* spirits involved in the situation.

CHAPTER

8

Becoming Spirit-Sensitive

"Beloved, believe not every spirit..."

If I were writing 1 John 4:1, I might have said, "Beloved, believe not every person, but try the preachers, the prophets, the teachers—whether they are of God, because many false prophets are gone out into the world." But the reason God says, "Believe not every *spirit*" is the fact that when a person opens his mouth to say something, a spirit is manifested. There is a spirit behind every telephone call you receive. It is either the Spirit of God, or a spirit of backbiting, a spirit of murmuring, a spirit of hatred, a spirit of gossip—some spirit is being manifested. Let's be a little more specific—every time *you* open *your* mouth, a spirit is being manifest! Most of us are always discerning whether someone else has a bad spirit; the place to begin the practice of discerning spirits is to test ourselves! Some people think they have the "gift of discernment," when actually they have the "gift of suspicion," or a critical spirit.

Notice, it says, "Try the *spirits*." When I first read this, I thought, "Lord, I don't mean to be disrespectful, but this sounds wrong to me. I know You're not wrong, but I don't understand it. It seems to me that You would say, 'Try the *doctrine*.' It seems that we should ask questions like: 'Do they believe in the deity of Jesus?' 'Do they believe in the blood atonement?' 'Do they believe in a bodily resurrection?' 'Do they believe in the verbal inspiration of the

Scripture?' 'Do they believe in the second coming of Christ?' I don't understand it."

But the Lord didn't say, (in this passage), "Try the doctrine"—He said, "Try the spirits." Furthermore, He spoke to me and said, "The spirit controls the doctrine." You see, we're one step deeper when we try the spirit. When someone receives a bad spirit, their doctrine changes. Eventually the bad spirit that is afflicting them will manifest itself through their doctrinal beliefs, and their doctrine will change.

What appears to be good doctrine is not always of the Holy Spirit. Did you know that the devil is very orthodox and conservative? He believes in the resurrection of Jesus; he's defeated by it. He believes in the blood atonement; the blood of Jesus is his worst enemy. I mention the blood of Jesus as I'm casting out demons, and I've heard voices speak out of people and say, "Don't say that! Don't say that!" The devil believes in the blood; he's a conservative. The Bible says the devil believes and trembles (James 2:19). The demons know they're going to hell and they shudder; they know hell is real. On one occasion they said to Jesus, "Have you come here to torment us before the time?" (Matthew 8:29). Those demons knew that they were going to a place of eternal torment and they were afraid of it. The difference in man is his ignorance and his pride; he isn't afraid. So you see, someone can be right in their doctrine and still not be of the Spirit of God. It's possible to be an orthodox conservative without being saved, just as it's possible to be a modernist, doctrinally speaking, without being saved.

"Try the spirits . . ." One clue to error and false teaching is the obsession to constantly repeat the same teaching or theme. Whenever anyone is into error or false teaching, no matter what text they take or what book they're teaching from, they always come back to that teaching. It seems to be all they can talk about, teach about, think about. For a dozen sermons in a row, that teaching slips in somewhere. The spirit that is in them controls them, and whenever they speak, out it comes with its teaching! It must manifest itself constantly. Sometimes the doctrinal issue involved may be seemingly minor.

If the spirit controlling a viewpoint asserts itself just ten minutes into a conversation, causing argument and strife, then it's not just a little difference anymore—it's a fighting spirit. It's an entirely different spirit, and that's when the problems come. Whenever we see the manifestation of a fighting spirit, we're not seeing the Spirit of God.

The Lord spoke to a dear brother who was really seeking the Lord about this thing recently, and said, "Whenever you hear a preacher being sarcastic, you can just put it down: it's not the Holy Spirit." Sarcasm is not listed as the fruit of the Spirit: "love, joy, peace, patience, kindness, goodness, faithfulness, gentleness, self-control..." (Galatians 5:22,23), and Jesus said, "So then, you will know them by their fruits" (Matthew 7:20 *NASB*). It is just as important to examine the fruit as the doctrine. Notice: Jesus did not say in this passage that you will know them by their doctrine—neither did He say that you will know them by their gifts. You don't test by the gifts, but by the fruit.

We need to become spirit-sensitive. For a long time, I never understood this, and I had to be "clobbered" and then healed before I knew the real meaning of spirit-sensitivity. As far back as I can remember, I had a happy childhood. I had good parents. I was never hurt by my parents; I never felt rejected. I always knew I was loved. Perhaps you have emotional scars from hurts you received years ago in childhood, but all I knew was love and trust.

I went through my schooling, college seminary—and

then came the ministry. I was preaching a revival in Minnesota, when a prophet laid hands on me and gave this prophecy: "The enemy hath been at work among the flock while thou hast been gone. Your wife's heart will be broken, and your mind will snap if you don't keep it fixed on Me."

So I returned home, to be present on Sunday (one day early) and that is when I discovered that a leading brother had taken the pulpit from the platform and placed it on the floor. He said to me, "We don't need an elevated ministry." He was one of my closest friends—my dearest brother in the Lord. It was so hard to believe. He sought to take over the church. You can lower a pulpit; but that doesn't lower the pride of the one behind the pulpit. If there's a problem, it's the heart behind the pulpit that needs to be humbled, not the pulpit. This incident really got to me; it wasn't just a feeling of discouragement; it was as if half of me was cut out and thrown away. It was really like a tractor pulling a deep-set plow right over my spirit. It was a rejection of *me*.

I wasn't as bitter as I was hurt—deeply hurt. I'm sure the devil would have liked to turn it into full-fledged bitterness. Remember that my first reaction was to say, "I don't care. I don't want to care. I don't care that I don't care—I'm leaving the ministry. I don't have to put up with it—I don't have to go through this." I was wounded in my spirit, but I knelt down in prayer and I told the Lord all about it and then came the choice to change. "Jesus, I don't care; I don't want to care; I don't care that I don't care, *but I know this isn't Your spirit controlling me and I choose for You to change me, even though I don't want to change.*"

I was overwhelmed with question after question. All kinds of possibilities flooded my mind. What steps should I take? I knelt to pray and the Lord answered, "You have one important decision: what are you going to preach about tonight? Don't make any other decision!" I obeyed the Lord and didn't think about anything else. The next morning the Lord spoke to me and said, "'Take no thought for tomorrow, for tomorrow shall take thought for the things of itself. Sufficient unto the day is the evil thereof.' Don't think more than twenty-four hours ahead." So—every day, I got up and made the decisions in reference to that day, not thinking more than twenty-four hours ahead, and it worked! I didn't have any problem; my mind was in perfect rest.

During this time, my wife was hurt over this more than I was, because she loves me so much. Sometimes when your husband or your children get hurt, it hurts you worse than it hurts them. In fact, Dee told me much later that she lifted her hands and praised God for six months in our church and never once felt the Holy Spirit. She's like that, anyway, though: when she makes up her mind to praise God, it doesn't make any difference whether she has an emotional response or not.

But, the reason I'm sharing this is that you can be healed, too—it can work for you. Some of you have been hurt by your husband, your wife, a relative, a neighbor, a preacher or a church member.

There are real problems that people face and they really do get hurt. The problems are not always demons; they may be wounds in the spirit that open that spirit to demons. You may be the innocent party to a situation where someone "does you dirty"—and the devil "gets his hook into you" through hatred. I've known people who were cheated out of money, or molested—absolutely the innocent party. And yet, through those incidents the devil got his hooks in them and they were filled with hatred. At this point, the devil was successful in controlling not only the perpetrator but the victim, and I can just see him sitting there and laughing—he *had* everybody concerned!

Remember that after Jesus healed me, what looked like the worst day in my life became a glorious day. I used to read the passage from the Sermon on the Mount: "Blessed are they that mourn" (Matthew 5:4), and think, "You've got to be kidding—that just can't be true!" Now I understand it. Through this deep trial Jesus had given me a brand new revelation of the hearts and needs of people. I became "spirit-sensitive" for the first time, and I could understand how other people were hurt. The Scriptures say that "sorrow is better than laughter" (Ecclesiastes 7:3), but it doesn't seem so until you read another verse that goes with it: ". . . weeping may endure for a night, but joy cometh in the morning" (Psalm 30:5). This was a difficult six-month period for me of sorrow and crying, but sometimes there has to be a "night of weeping." (It may last more than twenty-four hours.) Ever since that time, I've been spirit-sensitive.

Now, when I look at a person, I see their spirit—not the hair, the eyes—that's just their house. The real person is the spirit. Remember John 4:1—"Try the *spirits*." Look at the spirit of a preacher: is the love of God coming out of him? What he says may be correct, but if he's hating everybody, he has a wrong spirit. When however, you see someone manifesting the sweetness of Jesus, it's winsome, it's lovely, it's wonderful. I'd like to have met Jesus—not to see whether He had long hair or dark skin, but I'd like to have seen His Spirit in action in Jesus, the Man. But you see, I have that Jesus and I've met Him in a lot of others, and that's what you and I are both looking for—something more than correct doctrine. "Try the spirits." What kind of spirit does that church have? What kind of spirit is manifested at the Thursday morning Bible study? What spirit has that radio broadcast? What kind of spirit does that brother or sister have? What kind of spirit do *you* have? Most important, what kind of spirit do *I* have? I've seen some really beautiful human spirits,—spirits in harmony with the Spirit of God. Have you ever known someone like that? Have you ever known someone that was really homely, but when you got to know them they were beautiful? Or have you known someone who was physically beautiful, attractive, or handsome—but when you got to know them you found they were ugly?

A real mistake that young people make is picking out a spouse on the basis of the flesh. After marriage they can't stand the spirit inside of their mate. Their spirits clash—are incompatible. We're too flesh-centered. It's ridiculous to choose a marriage partner on the basis of their flesh. You may say, "Well, I don't like the spirit of the one I ended up with;" you're twenty years too late! You know what you can do about it? *You can bless into somebody what they're lacking.* If you see someone who's critical, begin to bless them with the spirit of sweetness. If they're sad, begin to bless them with the spirit of joy. I do this with my children all the time. One of my children used to be sad continually; I began to bless that child with joy (secretly), and that child is so happy now it's almost irritating!

Do you see what I mean about being spirit-sensitive? When you have been hurt, then you can see the hurt of someone else, and you can say, "Oh, God, I wish I could pray with that sister!" because now you can feel it. It's a wonderful thing to be sensitive to the human spirit of other people. It also works in reverse: it's much easier now for me to see when *I* hurt *others*. The average man isn't aware that he's hurting his wife by some of the things he says to her . . . it just doesn't even occur to him. But I know better now. Whenever I say something that hurts Dee, I can see the hurt in her eyes, and I immediately "cool it!" I also know what I do to my children. One night the family was having a little fun, and we began teasing one another—I guess you could have called it "foolish jesting." Finally, one of my daughters shouted, "Stop it!" The Lord immediately spoke to me, "You'd better lay off that child." And I can see that is how her problem could grow roots.

Now I know what Jesus meant when He said, "Father, forgive them; for they know not what they do" (Luke 23:34). Meditate on that for a moment: didn't they know what they were doing? They *knew* they were putting those nails in His hands. They *knew* they twisted that crown of thorns down on His head. They *knew* they scourged Him! How can Jesus say they didn't know what they did? They knew full well what they did! They knew what they did to His *body*—but they didn't understand what they did to His *spirit*. I, too, had to pray that prayer for that brother that hurt me. He didn't understand, either. "Father, forgive him for he didn't know what he did to my wife; he didn't know what he did to me." He was blind to what he was doing to my spirit.

The roots of our pains and anxieties are so important. Remember what the Lord spoke to me about "surface ministry,"—"You preach on the surface, people pray on the surface, and then get healed on the surface!" But, when you get to the root of the problem and pray, "Lord, I have hatred; wash that out of me with Your blood," you're applying the blood of Jesus to the root and you have real deliverance—salvation *below the surface*. Your whole attitude toward life changes.

A friend of mine and I ministered some time ago to a young man who told us, "I can't read the Bible." The Lord spoke to the brother ministering with me and said, "Third grade." So he asked, "What happened to you in the third grade?" The answer: "A teacher accused me of cheating when I didn't cheat so I just stood up, threw my books on the floor, and said, 'I'll never study again.'" We asked, "Did you forgive that teacher?" "No," he answered. We asked him to pray and forgive that teacher for accusing him of cheating when he hadn't. I told him, "You've got to repent of this—change your mind about it." (Recall that the word *repent* from the New Testament Greek means "to change your mind.") So he prayed, "Lord, I decided that day not to study. Now I change my mind—I repent of that decision and make another one: I choose to study anything that's truth." He was *free* from that point on to read the Scriptures. Do you see what happened? The salvation message got below the surface to the specific problem; then the blood of Jesus, forgiveness, and prayer was applied to the specific root problem. He was healed of the root and subsequently was saved from not being able to read the Scriptures.

I used to think that the psychiatrists' "problems-stemming-from-childhood" approach was a "bunch of baloney," but now I know better—I've prayed with too many people. Chances are, you're reading this book and have had problems of rejection. You're crying out for love, and perhaps never got it. You see, we're created in the image of God and His likeness. God needs love, and He wants love from someone who isn't forced to give it. That's why He created man—for fellowship, friendship, spontaneous love. You and I—all of us—were made in His likeness, and we're the same way. We want to be loved, appreciated, trusted for the individuals we are, the way we are. We want to be loved by someone who doesn't *have* to love us, but who *chooses* to love us. You do not have to apologize for wanting to be loved. God designed you that way!

Secondly, God wanted the fellowship of man so He could love man—pour out His love on him—bless him. It is the nature of God to give love, and that's inherent in

163

your nature also. You not only need to be loved; you need to love—to care for someone, love someone, pour out your blessings on someone. It's in the nature of God, and it's in your nature. Whether you're an eighty-five-year-old man, a five-week-old baby, a teenager, a middle-aged housewife or businessman, it's all the same.

When I was in college, we viewed a movie in psychology class of an experiment; a test. I don't approve of the test, but its results prove this point of needing love. The test was conducted with ten tiny babies. The babies were not hand-held or hand-fed or shown any love. They were provided with bottles propped up so they could eat. Their diapers were changed. Otherwise, they were totally ignored. Pictures were taken of each baby every day. What happened? They became pale. They lost weight. Every one of them was starving for love. You may say, "If they were so tiny, they wouldn't know the difference." I tell you, if a pregnant mother doesn't want the baby, that baby in the womb can feel the rejection. Furthermore, if a mother resents her newborn child, her milk can even make that baby sick. There's more need for love in children than most people will ever know. All of us need love. I want someone to love me all the time; you're the same way.

Some of you mothers say, "Being a woman is such a low calling." Your calling, Mother, is the crying heart of a little child, asking for your love. That is not a low calling; it's a beautiful thing. I tell you, Mother, yours is the highest calling in the world. If you can get a revelation of how desperately that five-year-old boy, that seven-year-old girl, that thirteen-year-old child needs your love and care, it will change your life. You might even quit your job. I don't believe in working mothers. I know sometimes its unavoidable, but how much is a *mother* worth? Five hundred dollars a month? My wife is worth more than five hundred dollars a month to my children any month of the year. "Well," you say, "we need the twenty-five dollars a month for the stereo and one hundred dollars a month for the car payment..." I ask you, wouldn't it be better if you let some of those things go? One reason mothers don't realize how important their place is, is because they think that to get down in the middle of the floor and play with the kids is too childish. No, it isn't. Spending time with those kids is your task and assignment. Baking cookies for them is another assignment! They'll never forget that. Mmmmm—Mommy's cookies! That's your calling.

Let's look in on a typical couple, Tom and Sally.

"What did you do today, Tom?"

"Well, I worked down at Colgate, clocked in and watched the gauges on this machine so it wouldn't blow up."

"Fine! Wonderful calling, Tom."

"What did you do today, Sally?"

"Oh, I just loved the kids and took care of them."
Now who had the higher calling? I tell you, God has honored you women in giving the responsibility and care of those children into your hands. He didn't put them in man's hands, primarily; He's honored *you* with that. I'm glad He's honored my wife that way. There's just no way that I could do what she does for our kids. They love her so much.

A mother may think, "Well, I could clean up the house in an hour and a half; then I wouldn't have anything to do." Do you realize that just spending time with those kids is what you're to do? Sure, you can clean the house in an hour and a half (I don't mean a good cleaning, I mean a "quickie.") But the reason you get bored is that you don't yet have the revelation that working with the children is your task. It seems like nothing important, but the very character and personality of those children are being formed and developed by Mother's relationship with them. So Mother, relax, stay home more, spend time with the kids! Don't run off to Bible studies, and don't leave your husband home alone, either. Go to church on Sunday, sure, but whenever you sense that your husband wants you by his side, you'd better be there! I don't care if you're sixty years old, you're your husband's sweetheart. Perhaps I'm digressing here, but the Scriptures say in 1 Timothy 3:2 that a bishop must be the husband of one wife. The literal rendering from the Greek is "a one-woman man." I've known men who were husband to one wife, but not a "one-woman man." My wife, Dee, is my woman—she's my sweetheart, and I still like Valentine's Day! And she makes that easy for me. You women can make it easier for your husbands to be a "one-woman man" by being sensitive to his spirit.

You mothers are working with lives, while we dads are working with things (usually). We bring in the income, but God has placed the children in your hands. I hope that encourages you to be a good mother and a good wife. Nothing is more important in life than relationships. That's what life is all about—relationships with people, and I can't begin to stress the importance of the one you have with your children, Mother.

One day three years ago, I was reading Hebrews 11:7.

> "By faith Noah, being warned of God of things not seen as yet, moved with fear, prepared an ark to the saving of his house..."

We were on a tight budget and I pastored a little church without sufficient income, so my wife worked three shifts a week. It started out as one day a week, then two, then three, until we were accustomed to the income and it was necessary. It seemed we were trapped in that situation. As I was reading Hebrews 11:7, God showed me things not seen as yet: dope in the schools, immorality, wickedness. Noah, too, saw the wickedness of his day and the coming judgment, and, moving with fear, prepared an ark. The Lord spoke to me; "I've shown you things not seen as yet and I want you to prepare an ark for the saving of your household. Noah didn't wait until the flood to build the ark. You start building your ark today. The first plank in that ark is to get your wife home with your children."

Notice the first two words in Hebrews 11:7: "By faith..." My wife made roughly $30 a shift, three shifts per week—a $360 loss per month. *That* kind of a move would *have* to be by faith! "Lord," I said, "there's just no way! But," I continued, "I tell You what, Lord; if You will raise my salary $25 a week, which is $100 a month (which any mathematician will tell you is *still* $260 short of the budget), I'll know this is of You, and I'll do it." So I began to fast. I had fasted for fourteen days when one of the elders approached me and said, "The elders have met privately, and we're raising your salary $25 a week. Not only that, I prayed for confirmation, opened my Bible and pointed to a verse for confirmation, and I pointed to verse 25 of that chapter. We know we're supposed to do it, because God spoke to another elder and told him to give you a raise of $25 a week."

Hallelujah! I explained it all to Dee, ending, "I want you to quit working." She had worked there seven years, had enjoyed the challenge, had made friends, and I didn't realize how much it meant to her life. However, she was submissive, and it was the wisest, most significant decision (outside of my salvation and baptism in the Holy Spirit) that I've ever made in my life. I can see the effect that decision has had on our children and the wonderful changes over the years. All four are teenagers now. The Lord has since that time spoken to me and said, "Is it worth $360 a month to you to have your wife home?" How can you put a price tag on that? We've got to get our values right.

So here you are, Mother, and you have two or three (or

more) little kiddies—they're either going to heaven or hell some day. There is nothing more valuable than those kids. You must be willing to drive a car that's five or six years old, if that's what it requires to have those kids properly trained and raised in the things of God. It's rough in the public schools today. The local schools here are besieged with dope and alcohol. I know the young people of this city, and I've talked and prayed with many of them. I know from their testimony that there isn't a child who isn't offered dope in one of the local high schools. In a day when the schools are flooded with dope and unbelief, the home has got to be twice as strong, "being warned of God of things not seen as yet!" It may get worse, but if that home is solid, then we've got something. Let's shore up the foundations of the home, starting with *our* generation—those of us in our 30's, 40's, or 50's, we're doped on materialism. Some of us are so doped—wanting houses, furniture, the place on the lake—we don't realize we've had our brains just as fried as the kid's brains on L.S.D. Let's get our priorities straight.

I've prayed with girls eighteen or nineteen years old who have said, "My daddy never held me on his lap or put his arm around me." I never want *my* girls to have to say that, so I go right home and put my arm around them and really let them know I love them. One time one of my daughters said to me, "Daddy, are we a bother to you?" I reassured her: "Not so!" So many kids are afraid to get married and have children because they have the impression that "having kids is a bummer!" Where did they get that from? From *us!* We should love those kids, for having children is a wonderful thing; I have four of the finest. I love them all dearly.

When do you need to get your home in order? Today! Start now! Don't wait until the flood comes. Don't wait until your boy is fifteen and the police call you and tell you they've picked him up on a charge of "possession of grass." You've waited too long to start building your ark then. Start when they're young—start now. Perhaps you wish you had read this ten years ago—give the book to someone who can benefit from a start now! Remember, too—God is faithful to answer your prayers, even if you start late!

Remember 1 John 4:1? "...try the spirits..." Watch the spirit of that child. You'll see warning signs in his spirit long before you get the call from the police. Keep a sharp lookout!

A final illustration: When driving on a multi-lane freeway, I always watch the front tire of the cars in the lanes next to me. You can see their wheel turn sooner than their fender. In this way, you have a split-second more warning that they are switching lanes. On one occasion this enabled me to avoid a very serious accident. In the same way, a person's spirit moves before a change in direction occurs. When a person's spirit changes, that person is inevitably going to change lanes. The spirit of a person controls his doctrine. If he is being controlled by the Holy Spirit, his doctrine will be truth. But if you see his spirit change, in a few months so will his convictions and lifestyle. It is inevitable. You can spot the change in spirit *before* you can discern the change in lifestyle or doctrine. The spirit of a person determines his convictions. For this reason, God says, test the spirits. This is the first and primary indicator of a persons spiritual condition.

I saw the spirit of one of our church leaders change recently, and it really concerned me deeply. I did some serious praying, and I saw that brother's spirit return to his former sweet self. It's so important to look at the spirit of people. We all need to be more spirit-sensitive.

CHAPTER

9

The Whole Man

> "For the word of God is living and active and sharper than any two-edged sword, and piercing as far as the division of soul and spirit, of both joints and marrow, and able to judge the thoughts and intentions of the heart" (Hebrews 4:12, *NASB*).

Before we can properly understand the enemy's attack of the Christian, it is necessary to examine the component structure of the Christian—to define and understand what we really are from the Word of God. Notice, God's Word is living, active, and sharper than a two-edged sword! That's why people don't read the Bible: they don't want to get pierced by finding out the truth; they'd rather hide, justify their sin, condone themselves. The Word of God cuts in and digs, piercing as far as "the division of soul and spirit." Other books may be inspirational or enlightening but the Word of God will pierce through you and reveal the truth. Notice, also, that it is able to judge the thoughts and intentions of the heart. I love this verse of Scripture. I have proved it true by opening the Bible and asking people if they intend to obey its instruction. When they answer, I hold them to the Word, and I will soon know the intentions of their hearts. When a person is confronted with Scripture that defines their problem, they reveal the heart's true condition by their reaction to the Word.

In light of Hebrews 4:12: "...piercing as far as the

division of soul and spirit..."—it is proper and very helpful to our Christian walk to make that division between soul and spirit, or between our spiritual and soulish realms.

> "Now may the God of peace Himself sanctify you entirely; and may your *spirit* and *soul* and *body* be preserved complete, without blame at the coming of our Lord Jesus Christ" (1 Thessalonians 5:23 *NASB*).

We'll never have peace without sanctification, and Paul's prayer is that God Himself would do a work that we can't do—that He'll sanctify us. This ought to be our prayer for our children, husband, wife, or those for whom we're responsible. Notice that He wants to sanctify us *entirely*—completely, taking in the whole scope of man: *spirit, soul,* and *body.* God always starts with the inside and works out—first your spirit, then your soulish realm, and finally your body. We usually say "body, soul, and spirit"—but the Bible says, "spirit, soul, and body."

Remember the prophecy God gave me? "Doctors start from the outside and work in"—that's true—they treat the physical; if that's unsuccessful, they send you to a psychiatrist. But the Lord's prophecy to me continued: "... but I am the Creator, and I start with the spirit and work out." When our spirit is right (with the hatred and the sin gone; at peace with God), then our mind will be whole, (our soulish realm will straighten out), and finally our body will be made whole.

God is a threefold Being, and we were created in His image—we have a body, a soulish realm (which includes our mind), and a spirit. By contrast, animals only have bodies and souls. They have a mind, some capability to think, reason, remember, and a consciousness of things around them. What separates them from man is their lack of a spirit, or God-consciousness. Animal is soul and body; man is spirit, soul, and body. This scripture in 1 Thessalonians 5 indicates a need for our sanctification in all three areas. Our spirit isn't perfect just because we're saved; otherwise it would be foolish for God to say, "...sanctify them in spirit..." We also need our minds and the soulish realm renewed. We know our bodies can experience sanctification.

It is common for Christians to think in terms of "spirit versus flesh." That's entirely understandable; Paul makes this distinction in Galatians 5:16-23:

16. But I say, walk by the Spirit, and you will not carry out the desire of the flesh.

17. For the flesh sets its desire against the Spirit, and the Spirit against the flesh; for these are in opposition to one another, so that you may not do the things that you please.

This, then, is a discussion of "spirit versus flesh," and he goes on to list in verse 19 the deeds of the flesh, so we will know perfectly well how to identify the manifestations of the flesh:

19. Now the deeds of the flesh are evident, which are: immorality, impurity, sensuality,

20. idolatory, sorcery, enemities, strife, jealousy, out-bursts of anger, disputes, dissensions, factions,

21. envyings, drunkenness, carousings; and things like these, of which I forewarn you just as I have forewarned you that those who practice such things shall not inherit the kingdom of God *(NASB)*.

But God doesn't leave us there, Hallelujah! He goes on to list for us the fruit of the Spirit:

22. But the fruit of the Spirit is love, joy, peace, longsuffering, gentleness, goodness, faith,

23. Meekness, temperance: against such there is no law.

So we conclude the obvious difference between the flesh and the spirit, but we need to see the soulish realm as well. It includes our will, our imagination, our desires and affections, our ability to reason, our memory.

The manifestations of the flesh and the spirit, and the contrast, is obvious, but there is an "inbetween land" of the soulish realm. Most of us know when we're "in the flesh." We can easily identify lust, arguing, envy, jealousy, fighting and hatred. We can spot fleshly things—adultery, sorcery—these things are blatantly obvious; even the sinner can see it if he'll admit it. Galatians 5:19 says, in fact, that it is "evident." Also, it's obvious what the fruit of the Spirit is—love, joy, peace are easy to spot, as well. However, the manifestations of the soulish realm are not necessarily things that are obviously sinful; neither are they from the spirit. They emanate from our will. They come from our mind, our reason, our desires. I believe that most people operate from the soulish realm ninety per cent of the time. They're not speaking by the Spirit, neither are they speaking from the fleshly motivation, but from their soulish realm—the will, the mind, the intellect and emotions. We must become more sensitive to the distinction between soul and spirit, even as God advises in Hebrews 4:12.

Let's take "witnessing," for example. I believe that much witnessing is done in the soulish realm. God didn't tell you to hand out that tract and there's no anointing on your doing so; yet to be "spiritual" you think it's necessary—someone told you to do street work and you'll feel guilty if you don't! Soulish evangelism is not a matter of willful sin—lusting and anger, for instance, isn't involved—but neither is the Holy Spirit! When the Holy Spirit leads you to witness—things are really going to pop!

The soulish realm comes from "self"—self-effort, self-desire, self-ego, self-drive, self-assertiveness,—self, self, self! When "self" does the witnessing, we're not necessarily in the flesh, but on the other hand, *we're doing it instead of God!* Other things can be soulish—worship, for instance. There's a lot of soulish worship, and there's even soulish prophecy—prophecies that don't come from the Holy Spirit, prophecies without anointing. They're dead words spoken out of self-will self-assertiveness, without anointing. When they're spoken out in the worship service, everyone knows they're soulish, because they fall on the service like a lead balloon—plop! By contrast, when the word of the Lord comes forth, we don't have to ask whether it was from the Lord, because it edifies, it builds up, it gives life; the anointing of the Holy Spirit in the prophecy and the spirit inside of us *meet!* Hallelujah! Glory! "That was *God!*"

Have you ever had a soulish conversation? You suddenly decide you'd rather be somewhere else and you try to get rid of that person, and from that point on you have a very soulish conversation. There is no obvious sin present—you're not really in the flesh—there's no argument, no hatred, no jealousy or fighting. There's no spirit there, either; you're not really loving that person. You're just saying,

"Yes, uh-huh."

"Well, no, not really."

"I guess so, yes, uh-huh. Excuse me, but..."

"Well, yes, but I'm running a little late, and..."

There's no love shown, is there? If the Spirit was there, there would be love, joy, and peace. You really weren't patient or longsuffering. But you weren't arguing or hateful, were you? That would put you in the fleshly realm of Galatians 5. So, you're in the inbetween land of the soulish realm.

What about the conversation in the home? Most of us would probably say, "Well, I'm in the flesh maybe a small percentage—we'll say five percent, and I'm in the Spirit maybe five percent. You know, I get impatient, I pop off, or I say something that's not right, and I *do* talk about the Lord, and to the Lord, a part of my day. I guess the other ninety percent of the time I'm just speaking—just words, you know—not much thought. Yak, yak."

Did you know it's possible for you to go all day

tomorrow without being in the flesh and yet without being in the Spirit? You're not sinning, true—not mad, not fighting, not lusting—that's really great! But self-will is in control—it's *your* intellect, *your* mind, *your* reasoning, *your* imagination. When I first saw this, I thought, "Oh, man! Ninety percent of the time I must be soulish!" We have a lot of teaching about walking in the Spirit, and staying out of the flesh, but what about the soulish realm? What *about* our mind, our will, our imagination, desires, affections, reasoning? Our minds are heavily involved in this soulish realm—the Greek word translated *soul* is *psyche* from which we get psychic or psychology. I repeat, it is proper and very helpful to our Christian walk to see the difference between spirit and soul, so that we don't spend all our time in the soulish realm.

Equally important, it is wrong to assume that everything that comes from the soulish realm is sinful! It is also wrong to assume that everything that comes from the physical realm is sinful! There is a *balance* involved.

> "Bless the Lord, O my soul: and all that is within me, bless his holy name" (Psalm 103:1).

Notice, here, a man's spirit saying, "Bless the Lord, oh my *soul*." Your mind, your will, and your intellect can praise God—in short, your soul can praise God! I'm not saying your spirit isn't involved. I believe here the spirit is saying, "Come on, soul, get with it!" The spirit is also saying, "and all that is within me"—that includes the body. We need a release of the whole man—the soul as well as the spirit.

> "And it came to pass, when he had made an end of speaking unto Saul, that the *soul* of Jonathan was knit with the *soul* of David, and Jonathan loved him as his *own soul*.
>
> And Saul took him that day, and would let him go no more home to his father's house.

Then Jonathan and David made a convenant, because he loved him as his *own soul*" (1 Samuel 18:1-3).

The relationship of Jonathan and David here was a beautiful and proper and godly relationship, and a necessary one that resulted in a convenant. The *soul* of Jonathan and the *soul* of David were knit together. It was not an evil thing: these two men loved each other!

Let's examine the three Greek words translated "love:" *eros, phileo,* and *agapeo.* These are verb forms. *Eros* should be properly translated physical love—not lust. *Phileo* should be translated friendship or companionship. *Agapeo:* (Or the noun form, agape) is the love of God. These represent the three realms—physical, soulish, and spiritual. You need to be able to express love to every single person in all three realms . . . remember, it's wrong to assume that everything in the soulish or physical realm is sinful. It isn't sinful, for example, for me to go up to a brother or sister and hug them with a holy embrace and tell them I love them; have them as a friend; and love them with the love of God—all three are involved. Bodily expression is there, friendship is there, and "agape" love is there. Some people are so "spiritual," they believe it's wrong to have sex in marriage! It is spiritual maturity to have the proper release in all three realms.

Why did Jesus call Himself the "Son of Man" instead of the "Son of God?" He was talking about His humanity. He could have said, "I'm the Son of God," but, being in a human body and realizing that *we* have to be in that human body, He said, "I'm the Son of Man," elevating Man in his humanity as He said that. So we need to understand the need for wholesome, soulish relationships. Our minds need to be involved in friendships, as well as our spirits. If you as a teenager want to go skating to develop friendships, that's normal and healthy. We need friendships where the love of God, the whole personality and body are involved in purity.

Now, how does the spirit fit in? Let's define the spirit in its proper, God-intended place: "the Holy Spirit in union with the human spirit."

> "But the one who joins himself to the Lord is one spirit with Him" (1 Corinthians 6:17 *NASB*).

When we are saved, the Holy Spirit is put into union with our spirit. The Bible says that if we're joined to the Lord, we're one spirit with Him. God's Divine order for the Christian is this: *the Holy Spirit in union with our spirit must control and bless the other two realms.* As long as our body, our mind, and our soul are under the control of our spirit (in union with the Holy Spirit), the bodily and soulish realms cannot manifest evil. The key issue, then, is, *"Which is in control?"* Some people's physical desires control their mind and spirit; with others, the mind controls the body and spirit. In the Christian conforming to God's standard, however, the human spirit (in union with the Holy Spirit) controls the soulish and the physical realms.

Let's consider another Scripture: Titus chapter 2, verses 2, 5, and 6:

> "Older men are to be temperate, dignified, *sensible* . . .
>
> "(young women are to be) *sensible* . . .
>
> "Likewise urge the young men to be *sensible*" *(NASB)*.

It was recently pointed out to me that the only word that occurs in each instance in Paul's advice to older men, young women, and young men, is the word "sensible." In the King James Version, in these three places, the same word is translated, instead, as "temperate" (aged men, verse 2), "discreet" (young women, verse 5), and "sober-minded" (young men, verse 6). However, in each verse the same Greek word is used, which means to be of a sound mind, or to be in one's right mind—to be "sane" or "sensible." God expects us to be sensible—in our right mind. Sometimes Christians are downright weird, spooky! Paul is saying, "You older men, be sensible! Have some horse sense! You women, be sensible! Be in your right mind! You young men, be sensible! Have some common sense! Have your head screwed on right!" What Paul is saying is relevant here: the "mind"—or soulish area—is not evil; it just needs the control of the spirit! Neither is the physical realm evil when under the control of the spirit.

There are some who believe that the only realm of life for the Christian is the spiritual realm. The only things they're comfortable doing are praying or having devotions. Anything else is soulish! Anything less is fleshly! The outcome of this attitude is to become insensible—weird! They've gone beyond dividing spirit and soul—they've *denied* the soul and the physical realms. The result of this attitude is to have an unsound mind—devoid of common sense.

There are ten dangers of becoming so "spirit-conscious" that you forget the soulish and physical realms.

(1) *Unteachableness.* If you're so super-spiritual, so heavenly, so "in-the-spirit" that you don't have your feet on the ground, then you won't listen to counsel, correction, or instruction from another. Ever met anyone like this? They've thrown away their minds, because "if it came from my mind, it has to be evil." Don't throw away your mind! Put it under subjection to your spirit.

If we become super-spiritual we will lose our kids. Let's listen to them: "Man, my mom goes to this and my dad goes to that—gone every night to another meeting. They never have time to talk to us. All they do is go to prayer meetings and leave us at home!"

When we are in the presence of such a "spiritual" person, we're tempted to think, "Who am I to even talk to

Sister X? She's so far ahead of me, I'm even embarrassed to open the Bible in front of her. Why, she's had so many visions and revelations..."

As soon as I read that David's and Jonathan's souls were knit together, operating in *phileo* love, that friendship love, I realized that if we have only *agape,* we're incomplete, unnatural. Let agape love *control* your phileo love and physical love, that's what God wants.

(2) *Out of touch.* Super-spiritual Christians cannot relate to life. This is serious: Spirit-filled Christians so taken with the spiritual realm that they're unable to handle normal, everyday problems, decisions, relationships, friendships. Yes, they're out of touch—up there in the heavenlies somewhere and unable to touch base with normal living.

We discussed spirit, soul, and body concepts at a city elders' retreat some time ago, and God began dropping things into my mind about our relationships. I want to tell you, we had a tremendous time together. We ended the retreat with a "David and Jonathan" communion service. The bread passed around the circle in one direction; the cup was sent in the other. As I passed the bread to the left, I told that brother what I appreciated about him. When the cup made its way to me I passed it to the brother on my right and told him what I appreciated about him. We were all crying on one another's shoulder with agape love *and* brotherly love...we hugged one another, crying and sobbing. It involved spirit, soul, and body. I felt like I was with "the eleven." It was a moving, "upper room" experience. Deep friendship, physical manifestation— under the control of God's Holy Spirit—it was beautiful. Thus God taught me something about balance—the need for the release of all three.

(3) *Severe introspection.* Preoccupation with the spiritual to the exclusion of the mind and body produces another symptom: one is continually "up tight."

"Am I in the Spirit?"

"Maybe I'm in the soulish realm—better watch it."

It gets so severe, these unfortunate ones can "lose their marbles!" They are unable to just relax and love and live, becoming mentally ill—always looking inside, always judging, always running themselves down. They can't enter into the rest of the Lord.

(4) *Judging others.* Introspection, judging self, leads to judging others. You meet one of these people and immediately, from his conversation, (especially about others), you can spot it:

"I'm sure that brother was speaking from his soul."

"I don't believe that's from the Spirit—that's just soulish." You can't even talk to these brethren. It's almost as if, in the back of their minds, they have a threefold "fill-in-the-blank" form by which to judge every statement you make—three lines in there to choose from. You say,

"Good morning!"

("Soulish.")

"How are you today?"

("I didn't feel the Spirit in that; that's *soulish*.")

They become mentally unbalanced, judging others, criticizing everyone. I've met people like that; you can't even talk to them because of the barrier they erect.

(5) *Religious bondage.* You can see how this leads into religion. When a person believes that the only valid realm for the Christian is the spiritual realm, he bites off a real chunk of responsibility, setting standards impossible to keep. He must continually be thinking,

"I've got to pray."

"I've got to fast."

"I'm not spiritual enough."

"I'm not doing enough."

Some charismatics have a mentality of works. *No matter how much they do, it is not enough.* Then other people do too much. We have a path to follow with a ditch on either side: laziness on one side and busyness on the other. The super-spiritual person feels responsibility for more than his calling, and off he goes into the spiritual busyness ditch! Perhaps your place is called, in the Body of Christ, the "middle toe," and you're trying to be the whole right leg! The Word says, "Study to be quiet" (1 Thessalonians 4:11), and there's the little toe handing out eighty-two tracts, thinking he should be teaching, wishing he could sing better, or thinking of forty-nine things that he should be doing. If God wants you to be a toe, be a toe! Forget about being the whole leg!

(6) *Becoming soulish.* This is a paradox—that a person can be so uptight, worrying whether he's in the soulish or spiritual realm, that he becomes soulish. Trying so hard to be spiritual, he ends up thinking all the time, and in fact becomes soulish—governed by his human intellect. He can't relax, and he'd be far better off to just love people and ask God to lead him in the flow of His Spirit. But that's too simple. Even though the Word says "The steps of a good man are ordered by the Lord" (Psalm 37:23), it's just too simple for some people So he gets into the soulish realm, trying to figure out continually whether he's spiritual, or whether his mind is leading him. Ironic, yes, but I've seen it happen.

(7 & 8) *Sectarian spirit, Self-righteousness.* The Greek word in Galatians 5:20 is literally translated, "party spirit." "My group is better than your group!" I've noticed very spiritual groups; some of them never smile; they're so sad you can hardly bear their company. They believe in holiness; they believe in the Bible—and that's good—but they're so stern and sad. Often they have an air of superiority: "Our group is better than your group—we're more spiritual than you are!"

(9) *Sadness.* A serious Christian is not a sad Christian. "You smile and laugh—you even joke—shame on you!

You mean you play croquet?!" Some are so spiritual they can't even play that game of croquet with the kids. The holiness is good, but we need balance. I've seen it in group after group—you can almost see that cloud of gloom settle down over them. God wants you to be a total person, happy, well-integrated and living the abundant life.

(10) *Twentieth-century gnosticism.* Gnosticism was a false teaching in the early church. (The book of Colossians was written partially to oppose this false teaching.) Gnosticism was dualism, putting the spirit in one realm, the material in the other, and saying that anything non-spiritual was evil. It involved a very wide separation of the spiritual and the material world. Everything material was evil—even your body. And, there is a modern-day perversion of dividing spirit and soul that is similar, a false teaching that anything physical or soulish is sinful.

Summary: It is proper and helpful to our Christian walk to make a division between our spirit and our soul, so that we're not just speaking from the soulish realm. It's wrong, however, to assume that anything connected with the soulish or physical realm is evil. God's desire is that our spirit be united with the Holy Spirit, controlling our mind (the soulish realm) and our body (the physical realm). *Which is in control?* Some people are controlled by the body; some by the mind; some by the spirit. It's a mistake to become the super-spiritual person who believes only in the spiritual realm, falling thereby into the above ten-fold error.

God wants us in normal relationships with our marriage partners, with our children, with people. There is a place for "phileo" love; there is a place for "eros" love (excluding lust)—there's a place for the whole man, including body, in the worship of God. We must worship

Him in spirit, but we're also told to love Him with our mind, our soul, and with all of our strength. Physically, we lift our hands so that we can become totally involved in the worship of God—the whole being under the control of the spirit.

Can other people live up to our religious bondages, our super-spiritual demands? That's an interesting question. I understand why others backslide—I really do. Sometimes we force people to backslide because we preach in such a way that they think they can't just be *a normal person under the control of the Holy Spirit.*

Let this chapter release you to be a free person—not free from the Holy Spirit, but free from religious bondage. What did Jesus mean when He said, "Be thou made *whole?*" (John 5:6, 14). He meant the whole man—spirit, soul, and body.

CHAPTER

10

Ye Are Gods

"30. I and my Father are one.

31. Then the Jews took up stones again to stone him.

32. Jesus answered them, Many good works have I showed you from my Father; for which of those works do ye stone me?

33. The Jews answered him, saying, For a good work we stone thee not; but for blasphemy; and because that thou, being a man, makest thyself God.

34. Jesus answered them, Is it not written in your law, I said, Ye are gods?

35. If he called them gods, unto whom the word of God came, and the Scripture cannot be broken;

36. Say ye of him, whom the Father hath sanctified, and sent into the world, Thou blasphemest; because I said, I am the Son of God?

37. If I do not the works of my Father, believe me not.

38. But if I do, though ye believe not me, believe the works; that ye may know, and believe, that the Father is in me, and I in him" (John 10:30-38).

Jesus makes an amazing claim to the unbelieving Jews. He says, "I and my Father are one." He openly claims Deity. Yet He doesn't say, "I and the Father are the same." The word "one" has two meanings: one in *unity,* and one in *number.* The Bible says, "The husband and wife are one" (Matthew 19:5). Obviously my wife and I are two persons, yet we're one: not in number, but in unity.

Old Testament Hebrew even has two separate words translated "one." When Abraham went up to offer Isaac, his *one* son, the Hebrew word indicates an absolute one in number. It is an entirely different word than that used in Deuteronomy 6:4, "Hear, O Israel: the LORD our God is *one* LORD." In this passage, the Hebrew word indicates not one in number, but one in unity.

Returning to John 10, Jesus is not saying that He and the Father are the same person. He was on earth, the Father was in heaven, and He wasn't practicing ventriloquism when He prayed and the Father answered.

I believe exactly what Peter said, that Jesus is the Christ, the *Son* of the living God, but He's not God the Father. He is one with God the Father in nature, spirit, essence, Deity; they're equal in Godness, but they're two separate persons. When we get to heaven we'll see God the Father and we'll see God the Son sitting on His right hand.

Now to the main point. When Jesus said, "I and the Father are one," the Jews became quite upset. They even picked up stones to stone Him. It's pretty obvious that these are unbelieving Jews. He is not addressing Himself to saints, but to people with rocks in their hands who intend to kill him. Then Jesus said (I'm paraphrasing), "It's written in the Old Testament (Psalm 82:6) in your law, *'ye are gods'* and the Scripture cannot be broken. So why are you wanting to stone me, whom the Father has sanctified and sent into the world, if I claim to be the Son of God?"

I read that verse one day in total bewilderment, then prayed, "God, I don't understand; it doesn't make sense to me. How in the world can You say to a bunch of unbelievers who are getting ready to stone You, 'You are gods?' Lord, I just don't understand that verse of Scripture and You're going to have to explain it to me." (By the way, if you don't understand parts of the Bible, don't let it trouble you—after all, *God* wrote it! If you don't understand the Book, the best thing to do is to check with the Author. Just pray—and a couple of weeks, or maybe six months later, God will open your eyes.)

Six months went by. I had completely forgotten about this bewildering verse, and about my prayer concerning its meaning. I was teaching a weekly Bible study to a small group in my church and we had diverged from the Scriptures to a discussion of predestination. One sister raised the question of "free will versus predestination." I confronted her: "Well, sister, you show me one verse in the Bible that says we have a free will," knowing full well that there isn't any verse that says that, in those exact words. She became frustrated, upset, and angry, and I realized we were becoming argumentative. So I apologized, "Look, sister, I'm sorry. I shouldn't have done that and now we're starting to argue over the Scriptures. I want to ask you for your forgiveness." When I said that, I heard the voice of God, louder than an audible voice. It was as if God, as He did with Moses and the ten commandments, took His finger and wrote, word by word across my heart. This is what God spoke to me: "*I will give you the verse; 'Ye are gods!'*" Instantly I understood what He meant in John 10:34. Everyone is a god in this sense: a god is someone who can make a decision which no one else can overrule.

For example, take Jesus' statement in John 14:6, "I am the way, the truth, and the life. No man comes to the Father but by Me." Now it doesn't make any difference whether you or I understand that, whether we agree with it, whether we like it, whether we think it's fair—God said it and it stands. If we don't like it, it's just too bad, because we can't overrule Jesus; He is God the Son.

You are the god of your life; you are the president of you. You can make whatever decisions you choose in reference to your life. Therefore, *you are personally responsible*. Jesus is speaking to lost people when He says, "It's written in your law, in your old Testament, in the Psalms, 'Ye are gods.' The Scripture cannot be broken." There is no other place in the Bible where this phrase is used, "The Scripture cannot be broken." God says, "You are gods and you can't break it." You are the master of you. You're the captain of your destiny. You are the god of you and you can't break it. You can't say, "The devil made me do it." If you lust, it's because you chose to lust. *You are personally responsible for your demons!* If Satan controls any area of your life—*you have given him that control.*

"I can't forgive!" That's a lie; the truth is that you won't *choose* to forgive. Forget the excuses such as, "Well, it's my environment. I'm trapped by the ghetto." Jesus was born in a manger, and He did pretty well. This verse of Scripture goes right against environmentalism. We are not controlled by your environment, we are controlled by our choices.

We never want to face that "It's *me,* oh Lord, standing in the need of prayer." We're always saying, "it's mom," or "it's dad," or "it's the devil," or "it's God's fault." No it isn't! We're the one who's to blame, and we're the one who has to repent. Jesus said, "You are a god, and you cannot break the Scripture." The reason the devil doesn't want us to see personal responsibility is that when we see it, it will bring us to repentance. We will no longer say or believe such statements as, "Well, it was the way my husband treated me," or "I went to that church and they hurt me so much." There have been millions of people hurt. It isn't what happens to us in life, but *it's our response and reaction* to what happens that counts.

Remember that two people can go through the same identical trial. One of them will become bitter, disillusioned, and go into sin. The other will become sensitive and be twice the woman or man of God later as a result of the same trial. It isn't the trial at all; it's the response, the reaction, the attitude. You are a god; you can choose what kind of attitude you want to have. The Bible says, "All things work together for good" (Romans 8:28). All those wounds, hurts, and scars are for your good.

I always think of Helen Keller in connection with this subject. She could have spent her life as nothing but a vegetable. Most people in her situation do that. But she made some decisions, some choices, and she became a blessing to everyone who knew her. It wasn't her environment, it was her reaction to her environment.

You remember my relating the story of how the brothers in my church hurt me—taking it upon themselves to symbolically remove the pulpit from the platform with the statement, "That's an elevated ministry; we don't need him." One of the brothers had taken over, claiming, "I'm a prophet. Unless you're all rebaptized in a certain way, you're going to miss the rapture." The unforgiveness settled in; I didn't have much of a church left. And remember, even though I didn't care, I prayed, "God, I *choose* for You to change me. Even though I do not want to change, I choose for You to do it in Jesus' name."

The amazing answer to my prayer was that Jesus did it. I had wanted to leave the ministry, saying, "I don't have to put up with this; I'm going to get a secular job. Good-by to that church—phooey on the whole bunch of them." But you see, when I prayed and made a *choice* for Jesus to change me, He did it, He healed me. I am still pastor of the same church.

Most people run instead of forgive, trying to run away from their problems. That's why preachers switch churches all the time—every time they are put in a place where they have to forgive someone, they leave instead of letting the cross do a work in them. That's why laymen bounce from church to church.

A couple of months later God gave me the opportunity to use my experience to help another. A lady in our church, who was separated from her husband, had been saved and filled with the Holy Spirit. Her husband wouldn't surrender to the Lordship of Jesus, and finally divorced her and married another woman. That sister was deeply hurt and I hadn't been able to help her. I had prayed with her and counseled her, but I was getting nowhere—until I went through my personal trial and understood the pain she was experiencing. God spoke to me one day when I was praying for her: "She was hurt in her spirit, just as you were." I called her and invited her to dinner that night with my wife and me.

Later that evening we discussed her situation. I said, "I could tell you just how you feel, because you see, it happened to me. You feel as if a tractor pulling a plow set as deeply as it can cut, ran right over your spirit. You feel like part of you was cut out and thrown away, and you don't care anymore, and you don't even want to care."

She began to cry. I advised her to kneel down and say, "Jesus, I don't even want to change, but I choose for You to do it." Then I told her how my wife had prayed and asked the blood of Jesus to cleanse the wounds away. She knelt down and prayed and God answered mightily. It was the turning point of her life. I couldn't have helped her at all if I hadn't gone through that trial. I had come through my trial a sensitive person and a sensitive pastor, as God continued to mold me into an effective servant.

If you are a god, then you can choose whether you're going to hate or forgive, whether you're going to be healed or feel sorry for yourself. We don't like to hear about personal responsibility, because it removes all our "cop-outs" and excuses and leaves us nowhere to go but to repentance. Flip Wilson has a very funny record, *The Devil Made Me Do It*. Part of the script concerns his wife buying a dress that she wasn't supposed to buy. It goes something like this, "I was just walking down the street. The devil said, 'You go in there and buy that dress!' The devil made me do it!" I have laughed over that record, but I want to tell you that the devil can't make you do anything. God *won't* make us be obedient; so certainly the devil *can't* force us to obey him. If we sin, it's because we chose to, and we're personally responsible for that sin. The devil can *tempt* us to lust, hate, feel sorry for ourselves, get in a bad mood, etc., but if we give in to it, *we* are responsible. All that the devil can do is tempt us. The response is ours and we'll have to stand judgment for it. *The choice is ours.* It is false teaching to say that the devil can *make* us do anything, unless we have *given* him some control.

It is also false teaching to corrupt the meaning of predestination and say that it's God's fault. "I was 'predestined' to be this way." What we're saying is, "It's *Your* fault, God!" What did Adam say when he sinned? "It's the woman that *You* gave me, God; it's Your fault and Eve's fault."

There are still people blaming God for their sins, yet the Bible clearly states, "God tempts no man." It is not God's fault; neither is it your wife's, or your husband's. You are personally responsible. You are the captain of your destiny. You make your choices and then you have to live with those choices.

In 2 Peter 3:9, the Word says, "The Lord is not slack concerning His promises as some men count slackness, but is longsuffering to usward, not willing that any should perish, but that all should come to repentance." It is not God's will that any should perish. Yet Judas did; Pilate did. It wasn't God's will that Judas go to hell. It wasn't

God's will that Pilate should perish. It was God's will that they should come to repentance, but they didn't (that we know of).

According to tradition, Pilate died in exile, in insanity. God had warned his wife through a dream to try to get hold of Pilate, but Pilate was a god. That is truly an awesome thought. Pilate stood face to face with Jesus. If he had been seeking Truth, there was Truth incarnate on display right before him. But he didn't want God, and God didn't force him to receive Him.

You can thumb your nose at God; you can close this book in disgust with the thought, "I don't care what that preacher says, I'm going to do what I want to do." And the only thing I can say to you is, "You are a god." If you want to renounce Jesus, if you want to live in sin, there is nothing anyone can do about it, except fast and pray for you. You're a god. *You* must make the decision—God won't decide for you; the devil can't. The choice is yours alone. Free will is scary, because ultimately we decide our destiny!

The most precious gift, other than salvation, from God to man is a part of His own sovereignty so that we can choose. God wants us to serve Him because we love Him, not out of force or coercion. Love demands freedom of choice. If we're forced to love God, it isn't love—we're made to do it. God created us as beings who don't have to love Him, but who may choose to. How amazing to realize that God surrendered part of His sovereignty and gave it to us. We must face the issue of personal responsibility with fear and trembling when we fully understand that although God will counsel and instruct, He will *never* make decisions for us.

The whole Bible presupposes the power to choose. "Put off the old man" (Ephesians 4:22). If that weren't possible, why in the world is God telling us to do it? "Put on the armour of God" (Ephesians 6:11). How can we put on the armour of God if we can't choose? If we couldn't choose to be obedient, why would any commandments be given? Underlying every verse of the Bible is the inference and assumption that we have the power to choose. There are also many verses of Scripture which state it outright.

When Moses came down from the mountain and saw the children of Israel dancing around the golden calf, he said, "Who is on the Lord's side?" In other words, he said, "We're going to choose up sides, boys, and I want to know who is going to stand with the Lord." And the ones who didn't—were slain. Deuteronomy 30 records Moses' last words to his people: "I call heaven and earth to record this day against you, but I have set before you life and death, blessing and a curse: therefore choose life..." Joshua's final words were similar, "Choose ye this day whom you will serve, but as for me and my house, we will serve the Lord" (Joshua 24:15). *He called the people to a choice!*

Jesus is calling all people to a choice. He said, "Narrow is the way that leads to life, and broad is the way that leads to destruction and many there be that go in thereat. Narrow is the way that leads to life, few there be that find it" (Matthew 7:13,14). We can choose which road we want, but the *end* of that road, its destiny, is *already determined*. If we choose the broad road, our end will be destruction; if we choose the narrow road, it will lead us to life.

Sometimes the choices which appear small and insignificant have eternal ramifications. In my own life, some minor decisions (as they seemed then) later proved to be major decisions which radically altered the direction of my life and my life style. (One such decision was the selling of my TV set seven years ago.)

One day, as I was praying with a long-haired boy who had a poor record of school attendance, I saw a vision in my mind's eye. The boy put his heel on a snake at his feet, but he didn't kill it. The snake pulled its head from underneath his heel in raging anger, viciously striking him again and again. I shared the vision with the boy and urged, "God wants you back at that high school. Don't skip school again. Go back to high school this very afternoon. Kill the snake—kill it now!"

He said, "No, I don't want to." He thought he was deciding only whether to go to school that afternoon, but in reality he was deciding which road he was taking. The boy didn't return to school that day. He dropped out of school, went into dope, and open sin and has never really walked with God since. The result of a seemingly insignificant choice one noon—whether to be obedient. He has only now begun to find his way back.

To Adam and Eve, it may have seemed a little choice whether to eat that forbidden fruit, but it cost them the Garden, and *life.* Someone may say, "Well, all I did was disobey." *All you did was disobey?!* It cost Adam and Eve the Garden when they disobeyed! We dare not disobey. Each of us right now is the sum total of the choices we have made. "Ye are gods," Jesus said, and you'll never break that Scripture.

Recall again the Gadarene demoniac, perhaps one of the most demonized men who ever lived on the planet earth. He was a violent, suicidal recluse who lived naked (the spirit of uncleanness) among the tombs. As Jesus came walking down that road, suddenly a naked, wild, screaming man dashed out of that cemetery towards Him. Yet this demonized man fell on his face and worshiped Jesus. Now you and I wouldn't have thought that that man had any desire for God. We'd have written him off as the most improbable and impossible case in all of Palestine to get saved. But even that demonized maniac still had his free will left intact. Jesus said "Go!" and the demons got up and left, and the man sat clothed in his right mind. What a marvelous deliverance! But the point that I'm making here is this: that man still had his free will. *God will never allow the devil to touch your free will—* that's your territory. You are the captain of your destiny. You are the god of you. You can look right into the Father's face and say, "I don't want You, God. And I don't want Your Son, and I don't want to be cleansed," and God won't stop you. Or, in all your affliction, you can fall at the feet of Jesus in repentance and be delivered. You are your own captain.

We must never let our circumstances be the focal point of our life or gain control of us. Romans 8:28 states, "And we know that all things work together for good to them that love God, to them who are the called according to his purpose." That verse doesn't say that everything *is* good; there are many things that aren't good. But it says, "... all things work together *for* good." God can even take bad and warped and sinful things and work them together for good. What happened to me in my church was sinful, not a good thing, but God worked it for good.

Most people misquote Romans 8:28 by leaving out the first three words, "And we *know* ..." You see, this wasn't theology to Paul; it was *life!* This was a man who was in a Philippian jail, falsely accused, his back bloody. I tell you, it hurts when someone accuses you when you're innocent. All he had done was tell that city about Jesus. As a result, he found himself in the inner jail, in stocks, with his back bleeding. Yet he and Silas began to worship and praise God. Because of their focus upon Jesus, instead of on their circumstances, the Philippian jailer was saved, a church was started, and we have the book of Philippians today. Paul could unequivocally say, "We *know* that all things work together for good ..." Many quote it, but they don't *know* it.

The last phrase of Romans 8:28 is often omitted also, "...to them that are called according to His purpose." What is the purpose of God? We find it stated in the following verse. "For whom He did foreknow, He also did predestinate to be conformed to the image of His Son..." God's purpose is that we should one day be like Jesus. Hallelujah! That's why we are confronted with all these situations. Why did I go through that trial? To make me sensitive and kind. Before I went through that trial and was spiritually and emotionally healed, my attitude toward someone who was having a problem was, "Well, she has problems. So what? We all have problems. Why doesn't she just blow it off? (An attitude all too common among us.) Once Jesus has healed you in your spirit, when you see someone suffering you can say, "Oh, God, I see the hurt in that brother and I wish I could pray with him." You have the compassion and sensitivity of Jesus instead of hardness.

Paul says God predestined us to be conformed to the image of Jesus. Examine Romans 8:29 closely. It doesn't say people are predestined to be saved. God foreknew 10,000,000 years ago that I would accept Jesus. He foreknew that; He didn't predestine it. He knew that *I* would make the choice. He says that everyone whom He foreknew to accept Jesus, He predestined to become like Jesus. They will be conformed to the image of His Son, that he might be the firstborn among many brethren. Why do we have trials? The Bible says that everything happens so that we might be conformed to the image of His Son. This isn't a predestination of salvation; it's a predestination of sanctification of the believer. The believer is predestined to be sanctified, not the sinner to be saved. The saint is predestined to be conformed to the image of Jesus. What a tremendous peace in the realization that everything that happens to us is to shape us into the image of His Son.

If we have chosen Jesus, we can either come easily or hard, but we're going to end up like Him. There are some believers who are like young heifers with all four legs spread out, braced, sliding and scooting and fighting the rope all the way up the hill. I don't want to be like that. I heard a preacher say one time, "I have never obeyed God unless He chastised me." I was sitting there on the platform when he said it, and I said silently, "God, I don't ever want to be like that. When You whisper, I want to jump—not balk. Just a whisper and I want to do it. I don't want to be rebellious and hardhearted, but a delight to You, Father. I want You to be able to look out of heaven and say, 'There's My child in whom I'm well pleased.'" I believe we should live so that God can look at us and say, "That's my daughter, I'm well pleased with her. She's a delight to Me; she's so obedient, every time I tell her to do something she does it." Praise God, you can be a delight to Him. Philippians 2:12 is a great incentive to this type of Christian life. "Wherefore, my beloved, as ye have always obeyed, not as in my presence only, but now much more in my absence, work out your own salvation with fear and trembling." God should be able to write to you, "Wherefore as you've always obeyed." If they did it in the early church, we can do it. Not just when the preacher is around. Paul says to the Philippians, "You're actually more obedient when I'm gone than when I'm there." I wish every preacher could say that.

He then continues, "Work out your own salvation with fear and trembling." He doesn't say work *for* your salvation, he says work it out. You have to have it before you can work it out. Work it out in how you treat your husband; how you work at the plant; how you talk to your children. Have you ever said to your child, "You never do anything right!?" Now stop a minute, that's nothing but a lie; you don't have any right to talk to your children that way. Don't lie to your children. Why don't you say, "Son, in this one area you seem to have difficulty." Don't exaggerate; don't condemn your children. Work out your salvation with fear and trembling; work it out in life's relationships. That shows we've got something to do; *that* is our responsibility.

But you must never read Philippians 2:12 without also reading Philippians 2:13. It is one of the most amazing verses in all the Bible. Verse 13 states, "It is God which worketh in you both to will and to do of his good pleasure." It is not our responsibility to *change* ourselves. It is our responsibility to *choose* to change and it's God's responsibility to *change* us. Here the Scriptures say that God will even change our will. If we choose to change, God will change our desires. All God needs is for us to specifically choose it in prayer. In fact, this verse states that He will give us both the desire and he'll also work in us the performance of the desire. He'll give us both the "will" and the "do." We may have said, "Well I just don't have any desire to stop this sin, or even to change my life." God says in effect, "I'll give you the will and then I'll perform that will through you." In other words it is by God's grace that we change. It is not our works. It is God's work through us. It is God who works in us both to will and to do his good pleasure. While the *choice* is our responsibility, the *ability to change* is given by the Holy Spirit. We choose and the mighty Holy Spirit is released by God to do the work within us!

The secret of prayer is that we can change. Through prayer our will can be changed. There is hope. The good news of prayer is that as we call on God, the Holy Spirit will come inside of us and do a work that we cannot do ourselves. The Holy Spirit is God's Agent to come inside of us, to answer what we prayed to the Father in Jesus' name. For example, suppose you have a long-standing hatred for your Aunt Margaret. You can say, "God, You know I hate her. I can't stand her, but I know this is sin and with Your blood, Jesus, wash it out of me. And God, in Jesus' name, give me Your love for Aunt Margaret. Amen." Prayer means you're not left to your own power, strength, or ability. "Whatever you ask the Father in Jesus' name, I will do it." God says, "*I* will do it." So after you've prayed, the Holy Spirit comes inside of you to actualize it, to bring it into reality. The next time you see Aunt Margaret, there is a love there. You've changed your will. How did you change your will? You confessed the truth to God instead of playing games and you asked Him in Jesus' name for love, and God gave it to you. He worked it into you.

The feeling that "I can't change" or "I can't forgive" is nothing but a lie from the devil. We are responsible for our attitudes, our habits, our life. The choice is ours. We are gods, and the Scripture cannot be broken. It is very significant that the only time the phrase "the Scripture cannot be broken" occurs is in this context. If there is any truth Satan would like to destroy, it is personal responsibility. The whole approach of much of modern sociology and psychology is that we are not responsible for our actions. Freudian psychology blames our wounds on the past, *as if we can't change.* This can be a royal cop-out. The Bible says, "old things have passed away." You cannot blame your environment, your childhood, your government, your parents, or your circumstances! You are to blame.

One day I was praying with a young married woman who was allowing her past to be her lord. She was another young girl who had gone through the unfortunate experience of being assaulted and this sad experience was controlling her life. As a result she had gone into adultery. She justified her sinful behavior by blaming God and by using her sad experience as a justification for her immorality. She said that since God didn't protect her and keep her out of the assault, she had a legitimate right to be immoral. As I counseled her, I asked, "Were you dating a non-Christian?"

She replied in the affirmative.

"Did you get yourself into a position of high potential?"

Again she replied in the affirmative.

I said, "Can you really blame God for the assault when you were dating a boy that was not saved, and allowed yourself to get into a circumstance that had high potential of resulting in fornication?"

She finally admitted that she was responsible for her action and her situation, not God.

The amazing thing was that she, because of having been morally attacked, would wear sloppy clothes, so that she would in no way be attractive to men. She also mistrusted all men. She hated sex and her own body. She had a man-hating spirit and an abnormal view point concerning her own body. I asked her, "How long are you going to allow the past to be your god? You're saying in effect, 'Jesus, get out of here. Jesus, I don't want You to be my Lord. The past is my lord. The past is going to tell me how to dress, how to respond, how to act, what kind of relationships I'm going to have with men, so Jesus, You're not my Lord, the past is.'" It was only when she realized that she was allowing a past event to run and ruin her life, that she began to change.

Unfortunately, many people are allowing the past to be their lord. A past hurt, a past wound, and bitterness has filled their lives and literally ruins them and dominates their actions. The past is not your lord; Jesus is! Quit letting your past lord it over your present, telling you how to respond. Stop letting your circumstances rule and reign over you; *you* rule and reign over your circumstances.

You are in control of your life, by the choices *you* make. Stop your pity-parties; be done with such foolishness. Stand up straight and tall and shout, "Jesus Christ is my Lord; I will not permit anything else to rule me." You are a god—you are responsible for you, and this truth cannot be broken. *You do the choosing, and God will do the changing!*

CHAPTER

11

Sanctification: The Will Of God

How often have you heard, or said yourself, "What is the will of God? I wish I knew what God's will is?" The Bible says, "For this is the will of God, even your sanctification, that ye should abstain from fornication: That everyone of you should know how to possess his vessel in sanctification and honor; not in the lust of concupiscence, even as the Gentiles which know not God: That no man go beyond and defraud his brother in any manner: because that the Lord is the avenger of all such, and as we also have forewarned you and testified. For God hath not called us unto uncleanness, but unto holiness. He therefore that despiseth, despiseth not man, but God, who hath also given unto us his Holy Spirit" (1 Thessalonians 4:3-8).

God's will for you and for me is sanctification. Paul closes this same epistle with a fervent prayer, "And the very God of peace sanctify you wholly; and I pray God your whole spirit and soul and body be preserved blameless unto the coming of our Lord Jesus Christ. Faithful is he that calleth you, who also will do it" (1 Thessalonians, 5:23,24). Hallelujah!

In some circles the word "sanctification" has almost acquired a derogatory inference. How unfortunate and off the mark this is. In the original Greek of the New Testament, the root verb "to sanctify" (hogiozo) means: to separate, to cleanse, to purify, or to make holy. The noun form of the same root verb is the word "saint." Therefore a saint is one who is separated from the world, who has been sanctified, i.e. cleansed, purified, made holy by Jesus Christ. By the very fact that New Testament terms refer to every Christian as a saint, we know that every Christian is to be sanctified, set-apart; a holy one.

In the Bible this word "sanctify" is used both of things and of people. When it was used with reference to a vessel of the temple, it meant that the vessel was set apart for a particular purpose. We can deduce, therefore, that sanctification is more than being separated *from* sin— hate, lust, depression, self-pity; it's being separated *to* Jesus Christ— *to* a ministry, *to* witnessing, *to* being a blessing to others. It's wonderful to be separated from sin but it's equally wonderful to be separated unto something.

First Thessalonians 4:3 states one particular sin that we are to avoid. "This is the will of God, even your sanctification, that you should abstain from fornication." The Greek word meaning fornication refers to sexual immorality in any form or description. It includes homosexuality, adultery, premarital relationships, indeed every type of sexual immorality. The next verse admonishes that *every one of us,* not just some of us, but all of us should know how to possess our vessels (i.e. our physical bodies) in sanctification and honor. God wants us to be sanctified in terms of purity and morals. We shouldn't be a dishonor to Christ. We shouldn't attend an X-rated, R-rated, or questionable movie. We shouldn't have filthy, dirty, pornographic literature in our homes. We shouldn't practice nasty habits or thoughts. Paul reminds us in 1 Corinthians 6:19, "What! know ye not that your body is the temple of the Holy Ghost?" When you got saved, your body got saved, too. Your body is God's property and it should not be abused or misused. It is God's temple. We should know how to possess our vessels in sanctification and honor, not in lust as those who know not God.

In the same context Paul continues, "Let no man go beyond and defraud his brother in any (literally: "this") matter because the Lord is the avenger of all such." In other words, he says that if we meddle with another brother's wife, God is the avenger. This is a stern warning from God. If we cheat or defraud our brother by meddling with his wife, we're going to have God to deal with, because God will avenge that brother. Are you surprised to find that in the Word?

"God hath not called us unto uncleanness, but unto holiness." Hallelujah! He has called us to holiness. If we despise this teaching, if we disregard it or set it aside or reject it, according to verse 8 we are not disregarding or rejecting man's ideas, but we are disregarding God. This is what the Scriptures say, and to go against this teaching is to go against God Himself.

Hebrews 10 illustrates sanctification as an experience, as part of the Atonement. Not only did the cross include the forgiveness of our sins, but through the cross we can also be sanctified. Old Testament sacrifices merely pointed to Christ. They brought fresh remembrance of sins to be atoned for, yet the blood of bulls and goats was powerless to *take away* our sins. When Jesus came into the world, it wasn't sacrifices that He wanted, but a body was prepared and that body was the body of Jesus. That body was prepared in the womb of the virgin Mary. The body of Jesus was the dwelling place of the Godhead and that body was prepared to be put on a cross as a sacrifice for our sin—as an atonement.

Jesus said, "I am come to do thy will, O God." How marvelous, how wonderful is our Lord! Let each of us desire that same attitude that Jesus had. God's will for

Jesus was to take away and annul the old covenant sacrifices, so that the new order might be established, by which we are sanctified through the offering of the body of Jesus Christ once for all. Hallelujah! By whose will? By our will? No! By Jesus Christ's will. Jesus Christ said, "It is my will, O Lord, to do your will." Because He willed to die, as a result of His will to lay down His life as an atonement, sanctification was provided in the blood of Jesus. We are sanctified by the will of Jesus. Not we "should be," or "could be," but we *are*. We are sanctified through the offering of the body of Jesus Christ.

How long does this sanctification last? It's *once* for *all*. Jesus didn't sit down until He was finished, but after He had offered this one single sacrifice for our sins which avails for all time, He sat down at the right hand of God to wait until His enemies be made His footstool. Hebrews 10:14 states that "by one offering he hath perfected forever them that are sanctified." The offering of Jesus Christ's body on the cross has perfected forever them that are sanctified. Sanctification is part of the work of Jesus on the cross. Hebrews 13:12 concurs, "Wherefore Jesus also, that he might sanctify the people with his own blood, suffered without the gates."

We are sanctified by His blood. If we want victory over a specific sin or habit or attitude or problem we wrestle with and battle continually, that victory comes through the body that was offered which sanctified us forever. If we will kneel down and pray, "That's what the Word says and I ask Your blood, Jesus, to wash that out of me. I claim my sanctification from that particular sin," then the blood of Jesus will sanctify us. The blood will wash it out of us. The blood will cleanse us from it. We will become separated *from* the sin and separated *unto* God. It makes no difference what our sin, habit, desire, or attitude is, we were sanctified once for all 2,000 years ago when Jesus

Christ died on the cross and shed His blood for us. It's part of the atonement. We don't have to go on sinning. We don't have to be defeated. We can have a victorious Christian life—not by our own works, but by the sanctification provided by the blood of Jesus Christ on the cross.

First Corinthians 1:30 assures us that "of him, (of God) are you in Christ Jesus, who is made unto us wisdom and righteousness and sanctification and redemption." Jesus Christ is made unto us four things: wisdom, righteousness, sanctification, and redemption. We ought to confess that Scripture right in the devil's face every single time we are tempted. If we are bothered by indecision, we can look up and say, "Jesus Christ, your Word says You are my wisdom. I claim You, Jesus, as my wisdom, my sanctification, my righteousness, my redemption." It's ours. It's already been provided by virtue of the cross, by virtue of the living Jesus Christ.

Our hearts are purified, according to Acts 15:9, by faith. There are many people who don't have victory because they don't believe they have it. So many people try to get victory by working for it, when the only way to be cleansed and set free is by faith. Your heart is purified by faith. That's good news. The Scriptures teach that your heart *can* be pure. And then God tells you how—by faith. Kneel down, ask the blood of Jesus to cleanse your specific sin out of you. Jesus will not only cleanse the sin away, but He'll even wash away the desire. He'll change your inner desires by His blood, and it's all by faith.

Paul asks a very important question in Romans chapter 6 verse 1, "What shall we say then? Shall we continue in sin that grace may abound?" What if one of you confronted me with that question right now, "Now that I'm a Christian, now that I'm saved, shall I continue in sin?" The answer is "God forbid." The literal Greek says *"may it never be."* May it never be that you continue in sin. "How shall we that are dead to sin live any longer therein?" Note that: Dead to sin. It is possible for you to be dead to sin this very day. "Know ye not, that so many of us as were baptized into Jesus Christ were baptized into his death. Therefore we are buried with Him by baptism into death: that like as Christ was raised up from the dead by the glory of the Father, even so we also should walk in newness of life. For if we have been planted together in the likeness of his death, we shall be also in the likeness of his resurrection: Knowing this, that our old man is crucified with him, that the body of sin might be destroyed, that henceforth we should not serve sin" (Romans 6:3-6).

Do you know what your old man is? I remember a lady who thought it meant her husband. And I've prayed with a number of young people who thought it was their daddy. But your old man is not your dad and it's not your husband. Are you acquainted with your old man? Your old man is that part of you which is selfish, lustful, touchy, dirty-minded, greedy, which complains, murmurs, likes to argue, fight, and cause strife. I'm sure you all recognize your old man! But what the average Christian does not know, is that his old man is crucified with Jesus. Your problem is not your sins, it is worse than that. Your problem is your sinful nature which *causes* you to sin. The sinful nature is like a tree. One branch is hate, one branch is selfishness, one branch is materialism, another branch is feeling sorry for yourself. Another branch might be cigarettes, and another wine. You can cut off the branches, but they always grow back. What you need is the whole filthy, ungodly tree pulled up by the roots and thrown away. Now if Jesus Christ did not take care of your old man on the cross, then His Atonement was not complete. If Jesus Christ did not take care of your old man on the cross, then you'll never get rid of him on your own. But this verse of Scripture says, "Knowing this, that our old man is crucified with him..." In other words, when Jesus died, not only were our sins put upon Him, but our filthy, rotten, ungodly nature was put upon Him also. It shakes me up when I realize that *my sin* was put on Jesus, but it literally makes me cry with anguish and joy at the same time when I think of the fact that this filthy, ungodly, rotten *me* was put on Jesus. The rottenness and the filthiness of any *one* of us was all it took to cause Him to be damned and rejected. The Scriptures say that our old man is crucified with Him. Christ was crucified 2,000 years ago. My old nature and your old nature were crucified 2,000 years ago.

A brother came to me after studying this Scripture and said, "Well, the Bible says I'm dead, but I sure don't feel dead. If my old nature is dead on the cross, why am I acting like I'm acting? I can't keep a clean mind; I'm troubled with dirty thoughts constantly."

I said to him "Brother, when did Christ die for your sins?"

He replied, "2,000 years ago."

"Brother, when were you forgiven?"

"When I knelt down and asked Jesus to cleanse me, I was forgiven. I felt that load go off my shoulders, and I was saved then."

"Now," I continued, "when was your old man put on Christ?"

"2,000 years ago, according to that verse."

"When will it happen to you?"

The man's face lit up with understanding and he joyously answered, "When I believe it." He immediatley knelt down and prayed, "Jesus, I believe what Your Word says, and it says right there that my old nature was crucified with You. And I believe it." At that point in his prayer, he clapped his hands and shouted, "I'm dead!"

"Well," I said, "Who's going to take the place of you on the inside then?"

And he said, "Jesus, You come in and live Your life through me and take the place of me on the inside."

He told me two years later that ever since that day we knelt before the Lord he has had victory over lust and has no longer been controlled by dirty thoughts. Hallelujah!

The ultimate in deliverance from demons is sanctification. We can compare demons to airplanes and the old nature to an airport. If we tear up the landing strip there won't be any place for the demons to land. If we are dead to lust, then how can we have a demon of lust? If we're dead to jealousy, how can we have a spirit of jealousy? Evil spirits attach themselves to the old nature. The Pharisees accused Jesus of performing miracles by Beelzebub. Do you know what "Beelzebub" means? It means "the lord of the flies." What a perfect illustration. Where do flies attach themselves? Not to a spotlessly clean vessel, but to a stinking pile of garbage. Our old natures are like a refuse heap and they draw flies . . . they attract demons. The best way to get rid of demons is to get rid of the old nature.

You may wonder: is sanctification an experience that happens to you once, or is it a process that goes on day by day? That's a very good question and the scriptural answer is that it is *both*. There is an initial *experience* of dying that creates a *process* of "reckoning yourself dead" every day.

For that young man that was an *experience* of sanctification. There was a certain point in time when he had a death experience. But it wasn't by "dying out," or by one day "laying it all on the altar" (which is works, not faith). One day he saw that Christ had done something more for him besides die for his sins. *He believed* it and he received more fully what Jesus had accomplished on the cross. Sanctification is not a result of *our* works, it is an acceptance of *His* work on the cross.

The Scriptures say that we are buried with Him by baptism unto death. Water baptism is a glorious funeral service. It's a funeral service for the old man. You don't bury something to kill it, you bury something because it has already died. You can be baptized until you're blue in the face, but it won't kill your old nature. But if you believe that Jesus Christ took care of your old nature on the cross, then you're ready for water baptism. You're ready for the funeral service at which your dead old nature is buried.

However, water baptism is not just a form or ceremony. God wants the heavens to open and the Spirit to come down upon us with the same spiritual significance as when Jesus was baptized. In fact, Colossians 2:12 indicates that God wants to "operate" upon us while we are being water baptized. As always the condition is faith. This is often the turning point in many Christians' lives. We have seen some believers delivered of cigarettes and other habits through their baptism. God intends water baptism to be the putting off of the body of the sins of the flesh by the circumcision of Christ (Colossians 2:11). If we make the decision, as an act of our will, to put off our old natures, God will circumcise us through water baptism.

Personally, I had such a glorious experience of sanctification that I tended to emphasize the experience rather than the new life. But the *experience* of sanctification issues us into a *life* of sanctification. The new birth is an experience which issues us into a walk. The baptism of the Holy Spirit is an experience which issues us into a life of progressive growth. Romans 6:6 states that our old nature was dealt a death blow 2,000 years ago on the cross. But just a few verses further, in verse 11, we are reminded, "Likewise reckon ye also yourselves dead indeed unto sin but alive unto God." That is something you have to do *continuously*.

I have already discussed the *experience* of sanctification as revealed in the Scriptures, and in personal example. Some scriptures set forth sanctification as an experience, while other verses definitely reveal progressive growth. There need be no dilemma here. We can and should believe both aspects: an *experience* initiating a *life* of growth.

2 Corinthians 3:18 gives us an excellent description of the life process of sanctification which issues from the experience. "We all, with open face beholding as in a glass of glory of the Lord, are changed into the same image from glory to glory, even as by the Spirit of the Lord." We are changed from one degree of glory to another degree of glory, as we behold the glory of the Lord reflected as in a mirror. That's a process. We should be a lot more glorious today than we were a year ago. With each passing day, we should become more filled with the glory of God and radiate more of the glory of God upon our faces. This scripture refers to an open face, an honest face. Are you open-faced before the Lord and before men? Don't try to hide things. When you confront the Lord with an open face, you'll start growing. Don't come to God and proclaim your righteousness. Just tell God the truth. If you're in trouble, tell Him so. If you don't feel like praying in the morning, just say, "Lord, I don't feel like talking to You today. This is a sin for me to feel this way. Wash it out of me with Your blood." Don't try to deceive God or yourself. Simply open up to God with open face beholding, and you'll be changed from glory to glory.

Sanctification was accomplished once, for all, by the offering of the body of Christ. Our sins and ungodly natures were put on the body of Christ, and through that sacrifice we are perfected. We must believe this every time we are tempted, continually reckon ourselves dead to sin and continually call upon God and present ourselves to Him with an open face.

My wife had been deeply hurt by someone's thoughtless comment. We have all had that experience and know the pain it can cause. A week after the incident she was doing the dishes and the Lord said to her, "I thought you were dead."

"I am," she replied in faith.

The Lord gently instructed, "Then reckon yourself dead to feeling sorry for yourself and being hurt."

She stopped doing dishes and said, "Lord, I do reckon myself dead to being hurt over this and dead to my feelings."

The Lord said, "Why didn't you do that right after it happened? You knew eventually you were going to have to reckon yourself dead, but you were miserable the whole week because you didn't do it right away. The next time, just as soon as temptation comes, say, 'I'm dead to that,' and then you won't have to suffer for a week."

This is the life side of the cross. Do you see it? Our old nature was put on the cross and we don't have to live in sin. But the devil, who is not dead, will try every trick to conceal this truth from us. Simply take your Biblical stand and position when you're tempted. Say, "I'm dead to that lust." "I'm dead to trying to be a big shot." "I'm dead to being hurt." "I'm dead to doing this for the wrong motive of getting attention." Reckon yourself dead every time Satan shows up.

If we don't reckon ourselves dead to spiritual or emotional wounds, we'll get sick. Hurt feelings bring physical sickness. We must reckon ourselves dead to them or suffer the expense of being weak and sickly. The Bible clearly states in 1 Corinthians 11:30 that if we have hurt feelings towards any of the Body of Christ while taking Communion, we will become weak and sickly. If you get mad at me, and I in turn get mad at you, we may both end up weak and sickly. This scripture doesn't refer only to our local church, but to anyone who loves Jesus, whether he be a Baptist, Lutheran, Presbyterian, Catholic, or Messianic Jew. Many, many people are sick because of resentment in their hearts toward a sister or brother in the Lord.

Is the teaching of sanctification condemnation or is it conviction? Does the preaching of holiness produce despair or does it produce encouragement? Jesus Christ, in the Sermon on the Mount, gives us three chapters of truth that we can't *begin* to keep on our own. Just think of it for a minute. "Be ye therefore perfect, even as your Father, which is in heaven is perfect." Is Jesus mocking us? Does Jesus want us guilty and under condemnation? Did Jesus tell us to be perfect just to make us feel bad and give us a guilt complex? That's what the psychiatrists say. They contend that Christianity is bad for man because it will just make him feel guilty all the time. I want to tell you that when Jesus Christ spoke the Sermon on the Mount, He knew we couldn't keep it. But He also knew that He would and did keep it, and that He would come inside us to keep it again. It's impossible to keep the Sermon on the Mount without Him. Christ has to do it again. "Christ in you the hope of glory." To me the teaching of holiness is a great encouragement. If God says, "Be ye holy, for I am holy," then I know it's possible, and I know that God wants to help me to do it. It encourages me; it doesn't beat me down. I say, "Hallelujah, maybe I fall short here, maybe I fail miserably there, but if Jesus demanded it of me, then Jesus will be my enablement also." "I can do all things through Christ who strengthens me" (Philippians 4:13). I call on Jesus Christ and I trust Jesus Christ to do the work in me—to make me the kind of husband, father, pastor, person I should be. Many people regard the teaching of holiness and sanctification with despair and view it as only condemnation. But it is part of the Good News. We can change! We can be like God, through Christ. And *the very fact that God demands it of us is an announcement that it's available for those who believe.*

Is sanctification just a tangent which some emphasize? Is it an obscure concept of the Scriptures which has been blown out of proportion by a few overzealous fanatics? Or is it the very fiber, the very core-truth of the gospel? I believe that Jesus, Paul, John, and God Himself say just what I've been saying in this chapter.

Throughout His teaching, our Lord stressed a life of holiness, of separation unto a life of righteousness. "Enter ye in at the strait gate: for wide is the gate, and broad is the way, that leadeth to destruction, and many there be which go in thereat: Because strait is the gate, and narrow is the way, which leadeth unto life, and few there be that find it" (Matthew 7:13 and 14). The consequences of ignoring holiness and continuing in a life of iniquity are clearly stated by Jesus in Matthew 7:21-23: "Not every one who says to Me, 'Lord, Lord,' will enter the kingdom of heaven; but he who does the will of My Father, who is in heaven. Many will say to Me on that day, 'Lord, Lord, did we not prophesy in Your name, and in Your name cast out demons, and in Your name perform many miracles?' And then I will declare to them, 'I never knew you; DEPART FROM ME, YOU WHO PRACTICE LAWLESSNESS'" *(NASB).* In Matthew 12 when Mary and Jesus' brothers sought to speak to Him, He firmly stated that "Whosoever shall do the will of my Father which is in heaven, the same is my brother, and sister, and mother."

We determined at the outset of this chapter that the will of God is indeed our sanctification. Paul boldly preached a life of sanctification. "Know ye not that the unrighteous shall not inherit the kingdom of God? Be not deceived: neither fornicators, nor idolators, nor adulterers, nor effeminate, nor abusers of themselves with mankind, nor thieves, nor covetous, nor drunkards, nor revilers, nor extortioners, shall inherit the kingdom of God. And such were some of you: but ye are washed, but ye are sanctified, but ye are justified in the name of the Lord Jesus and by the Spirit of our God" (1 Corinthians 6:9-11). "And they that are Christ's have crucified the flesh with affections and lusts" (Galatians 5:24). In Colossians 1:28, Paul states that his very purpose for preaching is sanctification. "Whom we preach, warning every man and teaching every man in all wisdom, that we may present every man perfect in Christ Jesus." Hallelujah!

John, the disciple of love, stresses throughout the book of 1 John that "Hereby we do know that we know him, if we keep his commandments." It is not profession from the mouth, but a life of holiness that really determines our relationship to God. 1 John 3:6-9 is particularly clear in the original Greek, stating that "Whosoever abideth in Him sinneth not (continually): whosoever (habitually) sinneth has not seen him, neither known him. Little children, let no man deceive you: he that doeth righteousness is righteous, even as he is righteous. He that committeth sin is of the devil for the devil sinneth from the beginning. For this purpose the Son of God was manifested, that he might destroy the works of the devil. Whosoever is born of God doth not commit sin (continue in a life of sin); for his seed remaineth in him: and he cannot sin (habitually), because he is born of God." A life which radiates holiness and righteousness is to be known as the child of God.

The entire book of Jude is stamped with the word

"holiness." It is only one chapter long. Sit down and read it through with the concept of sanctification in mind.

Then, turn to Revelation and read the awesome words of authority by Almighty God on His throne: "And he that sat upon the throne said, Behold, I make all things new. And he said unto me, Write: for these words are true and faithful. And he said unto me, It is done. I am Alpha and Omega, the beginning and the end. I will give unto him that is athirst of the fountain of the water of life freely. He that overcometh shall inherit all things; and I will be his God, and he shall be my son. But the fearful, and unbelieving, and the abominable, and murderers, and whoremongers, and sorcerers, and idolaters, and all liars, shall have their part in the lake which burneth with fire and brimstone: which is the second death" (Revelations 21:5-8). The words of God from His Throne breathe holiness. The teaching of sanctification is the very core of truth, it's not a tangent. Holiness and sanctification are a vital part of the gospel. "If any man be in Christ Jesus, he is a new creature" (2 Corinthians 5:17). Remember, sanctification is God's *divine will* for you.

CHAPTER

12

The "Way" Of The Cross

Recently a lady called me in reference to our radio broadcast and said, "Brother Gruen, I appreciated what you had to say about the cross; will you preach some more about the cross? We never hear enough about it—I'm hungering and hungering to hear the cross preached." I'm convinced that the Holy Spirit will anoint and bless any church that preaches the cross; He stands behind any group of people, church, or Bible study whose central message is the cross—not only the cross as it applies to Jesus, but as it applies to us. Hundreds of churches, preachers, and people will say, "Christ died for my sin," readily preaching that aspect of the cross, but they don't understand and have never experienced the work of the cross in their own lives. The cross is the very secret of the future of the Christian life. Paul said, "I am determined to know nothing among you save Jesus Christ, and Him crucified."

If we haven't learned what it means to die to self, be dead to sin, dead to our bad tempers, dead to lusts, dead to "telling people off," if we've not had a work of the cross of Christ in our lives, then we've not even begun to learn what it means to be Christians yet.

Every time the crowds got thick, Jesus preached the cross.

> "And he (Jesus) said to them all, If any man will come after me, let him deny himself, and take up his cross daily,

and follow me. For whosoever will save his life shall lose it: but whosoever will lose his life for my sake, the same shall save it. For what is a man advantaged, if he gain the whole world and lose himself, or be cast away? For whosoever shall be ashamed of me and of my words, of him shall the Son of man be ashamed, when he shall come in his own glory, and in his Father's, and of the holy angels. But I tell you of a truth, there be some standing here, which shall not taste of death, till they see the kingdom of God" (Luke 9:23-27). (Other gospels add, "till they see the kingdom of God come with power.")

You'll notice the context here in Luke 9 is the feeding of the five thousand. From the other Gospels we know that there were five thousand men, plus women and children, perhaps a crowd of fifteen thousand. Jesus had become popular in Palestine, and He's become popular in America. Chances are, if He were on television tonight, His message would be verse 23 of Luke 9. Notice this verse: He said to them "all"—preachers, elders, housewives, men, children, young people. You're not too young to hear the message of the cross. You're not too old to hear Jesus speak to you about the cross. You're not too spiritual to hear His words about the cross. If you're hopeless and destitute, you especially need to hear—you're never too wicked or beyond hope.

He said to them all, "If any man will come *after me*"—come forward and get saved? No! "If any man will come after me, let him deny himself, take up his cross daily and follow me." Three conditions: deny himself (not "deny things"), take up the cross daily and follow Him. If you follow Jesus, you'll be led to Calvary. There's no resurrection without death. Many want to be resurrected with Jesus, but they haven't died yet. It's a spiritual principle that death precedes resurrection.

"Whosoever shall save his life shall lose it: but whosoever will lose his life for my sake, the same shall save it." That includes us—that's not just for sinners. When we save our life for ourselves we lose the joy and the peace and the victory of the life of Christ. I'm not talking about losing our salvation, but losing the abundance of the life we have.

Jesus spoke to me and said, "The word 'dedicate' doesn't occur in the New Testament; I didn't say to 'surrender' either—*that* word doesn't occur in the New Testament either. To dedicate your life is a watered down substitute. To surrender your life is unscriptural." It's 'death' instead of 'dedication;' it's 'crucifixion' instead of 'surrender.' If you dedicate your life, it will last three days. If you have a bad day, it will last three hours. Jesus also said to me, "I want you to lose your life—throw it away and never find it again." Do you want to find life? Jesus said, "Lose it for me and for the gospel's sake, and you'll find it. Save it for yourself and you'll lose it."

As far back as high school days, I can remember how I used to think, "save, lose; lose, save—it's double talk—I don't understand it." And the Lord said to me, "Ernie, you're saving it for yourself, and you're losing it both now and forever. If you'll lose it for Me, you'll find it." This is an important truth; don't tune out this chapter! Our hearts can be changed if we don't let the devil make us apathetic. If we keep our lives for ourselves, we lose! It must be totally 100 percent losing it and never finding it again. Furthermore, we'll only be happy to the degree we lose it.

17. Brethren, join in following my example, and observe those who walk according to the pattern you have in us.
18. For many walk, of whom I often told you, and now tell you even weeping, that they are enemies of the cross of Christ,
19. whose end is destruction, whose god is their appetite, and whose glory is in their shame, who set their minds on earthly things (Philippians 3:17-19 *NASB*)

Notice in verse 19, Paul says, "If you're an enemy of the cross, your end is destruction." What does he mean by "enemy of the cross?" The enemies are not few (I wish he had said few), but he says "many" in verse 18. They're revealed by their walk, not their talk. "For many *walk* ..." in verse 18. Paul wept over it; it made him cry; it's a serious business. They come to church, they look spiritual, but when I look at their walk, they're enemies of the cross.

Here he is not speaking of someone who preaches against the blood; there are many who believe in the blood atonement who are enemies of the cross. They like to hear that Jesus died for them, but they don't like to hear that they must die for Christ. When you preach that Christ died for them, the work of the cross—ohhh, that's good! But when you plead, "Let the cross of Christ do a work in you," they are enemies. A friend of mine shared this concept with a fellow, and immediatley his eyebrows shot up and he got alarmed and agitated. That man is an enemy of the cross of Christ. We need an experience of crucifixion of the old nature and a sanctification experience. The cross has to do a work in us. If we're an enemy of that message, our end is destruction, our god is our physical appetites, our glory is our shame, and we mind earthly things.

It's good to look at the end of the road we're on. If we don't want to hear about the cross as it applies to us, our end is going to be destruction because we're playing games with sin and we're not real. In this case, our god would be our physical appetites, and we would glory in our shame according to the Word. I've known a lot of people who glory in how much they can cuss, how much whiskey they can drink, how much adultery they can commit, how many times they've shot up dope ... they glory in their shame. They ought to fall on their faces and

222

be ashamed to even look up at the Son of God, instead of blaspheming His name.

> "He made known his ways unto Moses, his acts unto the children of Israel," (Psalm 103:7).

Moses understood some things the Israelites didn't. For example, when they walked through the Red Sea on dry ground, all the children of Israel saw the act, but they forgot it in a short time. However, there were a few who saw the ways of God, as Moses did. They saw more than just the physical act of what happened, they saw the principles involved, as in the faith principle of stepping into the water before it rolls back. There are people who have seen miracles without seeing the God of miracles, and the benefit lasted less than a week: someone who has been healed, and is drunk a week later. Paul saw this kind of thing; no wonder he wept. They see the act, but they don't see "the way" revealed in the act.

Everyone sees the act of the cross, that Christ died for our sins, and I don't want to detract from that. Hallelujah for the most glorious act in history! There are some, however, who see the cross not only as an act, but a way of life, a pattern, an example. We must see it, too. What does it mean to take up our cross daily? It means we do just what Jesus did—what the cross meant to Jesus is what it must mean to us. I want to list eight things about the cross of Christ that need to be true of us and our cross.

(1) *He gave up His will.* In the Garden of Gethsemane, He faced the cross. He was fully prepared for the physical aspect of it, but when He faced the horror of that cup full of our sin and shame and filth—all the sin of all the ages coming upon Him, separating Him totally from the Father—damned, He cried out, "Father, if it be possible, take this cup away" (Matthew 26:39). He realized, however, that there was no other way for mankind to be

saved except that He die—be damned. And later, at the cross, when He cried out, "My God, My God, why have You forsaken Me?" He was totally cut off from the Father—He looked up and *God was gone*. He chose to take that cup; He gave up His will.

What does it mean to take up your cross? It means that there will be situations in your life where you'll have to drink a bitter cup that you don't deserve. I find that the person who is willing to bend his will to another is so rare that it's shocking; it almost scares me. Oh, how sweet we are when we get our way; how full of the Holy Spirit when everything lines up the way we want it. But what if we have to drink a cup we don't want? What if we have to give up our will in order to make our wife happy, in order to obey our parents—then it's a different thing! Oh, Christian, take up the cross! You say, "Being a Christian doesn't mean that!" But that's precisely what it means—to deny yourself and your own will. None of us have the capacity to bend our wills of ourselves, but few of us exercise the power to let Christ do it, either. I know of a husband and wife who wouldn't bend their wills: he wouldn't bend his will to love his wife, make her happy—no love of Jesus for her at all. She wouldn't bend her will to be submissive. If either of them had just given an inch, they could've been so happy, but they ended the relationship in a divorce court. Spirit-baptized Christians in divorce court? Neither of them would bend their will one inch. "Take up your cross and follow me—daily."

(2) *It was voluntary with Jesus*. He said "Take it up"—it's not something that comes upon you. When you fall off a horse and break your wrist, that's not a cross—it's a trial or a burden. A cross is something you voluntarily choose because of your love for Jesus—it's something you can avoid, but because of your love for Him, you choose not to get out of it. Examples: staying home when you'd rather go out some night because Dad asked you not to

go; staying married to a husband who doesn't treat you with the tenderness and sweetness you'd like (because you love Jesus Christ and you want to be obedient to His Word.) You could choose the divorce court, but because of Jesus, you bear the cross and let people say what they will. I know a lot of people who could get delivered out of certain situations, but because they love Jesus, they take up their cross—"Not accepting deliverance; that they might obtain a better resurrection" (Hebrews 11:35).

(3) Like a lamb before the shearers, *Jesus kept His mouth shut and didn't defend Himself.* There He stood, perfectly innocent, and when they spit on Him, He just kept His mouth shut. I marvel that Jesus didn't defend Himself. Most of the time, when people are accused, it's like pulling a tail feather out of a chicken: "Squawk, squawk, squawk!" I've heard myself do it. But one day, one of my daughters caught me reaching into a serving bowl of food with my fork instead of using the service spoon, and she said, "Daddy, you preach to us about that, and now you're doing it—you don't practice what you preach." You know what I said?—the only thing I could say, "I'm guilty." A funny thing happened—my daughter was satisfied, and peace resulted. That's one of the few illustrations I can think of in my life when I didn't try to defend myself. It's a wonderful thing to say, "I'm guilty, I spoke out of turn, I was wrong." Deny your right to defend yourself—that's a work of the cross in your life. The most irritating thing in the world is to be falsely accused. Many people say, "I don't mind getting blamed when I did it, but I'm just not going to take it when I'm innocent." Jesus did, and that's part of the cross. Part of the cross is also realizing that when we take up our own defense, that's where the Father *drops* our defense! If we'll leave the vengeance and defense and our honor and our good name to Him, He'll take good care of it.

(4) *He was betrayed by those closest to Him.* That's a

tough one: His best friends, His closest associates, they all left Him, but He went on. When everyone else goes back to dope, rock music and immorality, who cares? If *your best friend* betrays you, you go on! That's part of the cross.

(5) *He suffered at the whipping post.* Have you ever said, "I'll not be anybody's whipping boy!?" You will if you're going to follow Christ. You may be innocent, misunderstood. Your parents, your husband, or your wife lash out at you all the time—if not with the scourge, with the tongue. Some of you literally suffer at the whipping post . . . that's a part of the cross.

(6) *He was unappreciated* . . . think of His reward . . . a crown of thorns. It must have been hard for the very Creator, the very Son of God, coming to die for the sins of the world, to see some smart aleck soldier approach Him with a mass of thorns and say, "Here's your crown!" He certainly wasn't appreciated—instead of a "Thank you" He got the biggest slap in the face you can ask—blood trickling down His forehead. Today, if someone doesn't say "thank you" we're offended for six months. Then we say we're "filled with the Spirit." We have a long way to go, don't we, dear reader? They returned *His* good with evil; could *you* take that? Yes, you can—by His grace, you can grow to that. I've seen a few saints do it. Lord, give us grace to not only hear this, but do it.

(7) *He refused the sponge.* The vinegar they offered Him on that sponge was an antiseptic and He refused it. He refused to alleviate the pain of His death in any way. Most of us, however, look for any possible means to alleviate the pain of a trial we're going through or a cross we've chosen to take. I remember a particular cross I had taken and its pain. I shared that cross with two or three others on the phone and I told them "how rough I had it," and how I was being mistreated. Oh, how I got their

sympathy! Then the Lord showed me what is meant by "sucking the sponge," and He said to me, "When you took that cross, they stuck that sponge up to you, and you sucked it for all it was worth!" Taking up the cross isn't gossiping, looking for self-pity, telling everyone how bad things are, or getting on the phone and saying, "Hey, let me cry on your shoulder while you pat me on the back . . ." All those things are "sucking the sponge"—any old thing to alleviate the pain. Jesus did nothing to alleviate the pain. God wants us to go through it without one word of gossip. "If any man will come after me, let him deny himself . . ."

(8) *Pure anguish.* How else could you describe the crucifixion of Jesus? It was mental, emotional, spiritual and physical pain. Sometimes we think so much of His atonement for sin that we forget the nails in His hands—real nails! He was really in great physical pain!

"My husband beats me up; you don't expect me to *stay* with him, do you?" Jesus says, "If any man will come after me, let him deny himself . . ."

"You don't expect me to stay with someone I'm not happy with, do you?" Jesus answers, "Let him deny himself daily, and take up his cross daily."

"But I go through this every day!"

Again, Jesus says, "Take up the cross daily, and follow me!"

"But I'm in pure anguish! I'm going to file for mental cruelty!" Jesus, too, went through pure anguish. Some of you are in heartbreaking situations . . . situations that are unhappy, not funny, not good—you feel like crying—you may cry a lot. Are you going to run from it? Or are you going to pray through it? Would you escape your cross? You can you know—you don't have to take it up. It's up to you, but "if any man will come after Me, let him deny himself and take up his cross."

"I'm not going to submit to my husband; why, he's not spiritual!"

Jesus submitted Himself all the way to death at the hands of unspiritual men for the sins of all of unspiritual mankind. "If any man will come after me, let him deny himself, take up his cross daily, and follow me."

And finally, Jesus died. He died! If we're to follow Christ, we must die—death! We must be dead to the desire to "read the riot act" to someone; dead to being jealous; dead to throwing past sins up in another's face. Let's read the account of Calvary's hill again and follow Him to death. Let's quit babying ourselves, be done with self-pity, take up our cross voluntarily and follow Him.

But remember that with the cross comes the resurrection and that all suffering lasts but for a season. So, praise the Lord! Jesus rose again and sits at the right hand of God as our High Priest. "Wherefore He is able to save them to the uttermost that come unto God by him, seeing he ever liveth to make intercession for them" (Hebrews 7:25).

Only Jesus' earthly ministry ended when He died. His heavenly ministry continues as He prays for us; and *His* prayers are answered! Right now, Jesus, the Son of God, is praying for you in heaven. Praise God for the grace that comes to us as a result of His prayers in heaven on our behalf. Truly, we are saved by grace and kept by grace because of the risen Christ's intercession. We are going to be saved to the uttermost. Because of His prayers we can and will go the "way" of the cross!

One last word of encouragement. When Peter was proclaiming that he would never deny Jesus and would even die before he would disown the Master, the Lord said to him, "Before the cock crows two times, you will deny me three times." But at that point, Jesus knew more than the fact that Peter would fail. He also knew the power of His own prayers. Therefore, Jesus prophesied Peter's victory even before his failure, when he said, "Satan hath desired to have you, that he may sift you as wheat: but I have prayed for thee, that thy faith fail not" (Luke 22:31-32). Right now, in heaven, Jesus is praying for you that your faith fail not. Because of this divine fact, you will be saved to the uttermost. The risen Lord lives in you by His Spirit and intercedes for you at the Father's right hand—*that is double grace!*

Be willing to follow Jesus to the cross—resurrection into new life awaits you!

13

Grace: The Final Word

The moon-walks of our astronauts represent an amazing accomplishment in space travel, but that doesn't thrill me nearly so much as to think that my Savior, the Lord Jesus, took an earth walk. He came down out of heaven and left all of His riches in glory that He might become a man. Wonder of wonders, He did so that He might take that walk up the hill of Golgotha and hang on that cross to die for our sin. He became man that we might become sons of God. Hallelujah! That's what I'm thrilled about. He was rich and yet He became poor that we, through His poverty, might be made rich—rich with joy, rich with peace, rich with holiness.

This chapter is to be a source of encouragement. In the final ananlysis our entire walk with Christ is based on the grace of God. The Bible says, "He brought me up out of a horrible pit..." (Psalm 40:2). Suppose you were in quicksand, in a horrible pit, and felt yourself sinking lower every day. Perhaps the quicksand is dope, perhaps it's lust, or a love of money; maybe it's just that you're fed up with yourself, you don't like the way you're living, and spiritually speaking you're in a pit of quicksand. One thing is certain: your deliverance from that pit will not come from concentrating on the quicksand. You will only see yourself sinking deeper and deeper. You need to *focus your attention on your Savior, on Jesus*. If you look at your sin, you'll never be saved. You must raise your sight to the One who loved you enough that though He was rich, with all the glory of heaven, He forsook it all to become a man, that you and I through His poverty might be made rich. We who were lost in sin and trapped with our own chains of sin can be made clean and pure like He is, *as clean as Jesus himself through His blood.* We can be made rich!

One of the greatest riches we can have is peace of mind. Therefore to be able to look in a mirror in the morning and say, "All is well with my soul. Praise the Lord, I'm clean. My sin is gone!" What other riches can compare with that? Though He was rich, yet for our sake He became poor.

"You know the grace of our Lord Jesus Christ..." There are many ways of defining grace, the most concise probably being "the unmerited favor of God." Someone has said, "Grace is getting what you *don't* deserve, and mercy is not getting what you *do* deserve." There is not one of us who *deserves* to be saved. None of us are good enough in ourselves. Not one of us could earn God's favor or please God by our works. He *gives* us salvation. He *gives* His love. He *gives* us forgiveness. He *gives* us victory. We *deserve* hell, we *deserve* the lake; and yet God *gives* us His Spirit, His forgiveness, His nature, His gifts, and His fruit. We don't begin to deserve any of it. It is purely God's grace.

Someone has devised a very beautiful and concise acrostic from the word grace.

G—God's
R—Riches
A—At
C—Christ's
E—Expense

Grace is free to us, but it cost God His Son. It cost us nothing, but it cost God everything. He had to watch His

Son die for our sin. He had to watch all of our filth and rottenness and our sin put upon His spotless, holy Son. And when Jesus was clothed with our base and evil nature, the Father had to turn His back on His only Son. Our Savior had to cry out, "My God, My God why have You forsaken me?" It cost God plenty for our salvation: God's riches at Christ's expense.

This Bible definition of grace is not an intellectual definition, nor a lexicon definition. What is the grace of our Lord Jesus Christ? "That, though He was rich, yet for your sakes he became poor, that you through his poverty might be made rich." Jesus left all His riches that we might receive them. Praise the Lord! That's what grace is. The marvelous grace of God, that we who were sinners got picked up out of the pit and made saints.

Let me explain this salvation, which by God's grace, we are freely given. Salvation is Jesus Christ being put inside you. It is not shaking a preacher's hand or joining a church. It is not even being water-baptized or taking communion or participating in sacraments. Salvation is Jesus in you. You can be a preacher, but if you don't have Jesus in you, you're lost. The Bible says, "He that hath the Son, hath life and he that hath not the Son of God, hath not life" (1 John 5:12). Many people have church membership, water baptism, sacraments, even degrees in theology, but they don't yet have Jesus dwelling in them. I am not speaking figuratively. I personally know the day and the hour when Jesus was put inside me by God. It is an event which actually happened. Every person who is truly saved has another spirit inside him besides his human spirit. This is what Jesus meant when He said, "You must be born again." I am amazed that Jesus would consider becoming a man, but I'm even more amazed that the Holy Spirit would consider living inside of *me*. That Jesus would come to a cradle is wondrous, but that God would make me His habitation, that's tremendous! But that is what salvation is all about—it's God offering to make you His dwelling place. It is God offering to put His Spirit inside you. Every person must choose what spirit they want to guide them: an evil spirit or the Holy Spirit.

What comprised the riches of Jesus? We know those riches do not refer to material possessions. The riches of Jesus are found in His very nature, in His personality. Suppose I said to you this morning, "You can be just like Jesus." How would you respond to an offer whereby you might have His tenderness, His patience, His love for all people, His pure and holy nature? The greatest riches that God has are His nature and his Spirit. When God couldn't think of anything better to give us, He gave us Himself. At the moment of salvation, He puts His Spirit inside of us. The whole point of salvation is that you and I can be like Jesus. Hallelujah! The good news is that God wants to transform every one of us by putting the Spirit of Jesus in our innermost being. When we receive Jesus inside us, then and only then can we begin to act like Him. *We must have His Spirit before we can keep the Words that His Spirit wrote.* Show me someone, a woman or a man, who is like Jesus, and I'll show you someone who is the richest person in the world. "You know the grace of our Lord Jesus Christ, that though He was rich, yet for your sakes He became poor, that you through His poverty might be made rich."

There is a principle in that verse. Sometimes we have to let our riches go in order to make other people rich. Sometimes we have to go to a cross, not get our way, and be willing to give up our riches. The cross is not only the way of atonement, it's a way of living. Often we can make someone else rich by being dead to such things as retaliation and revenge. Next time refrain from giving someone your two cents' worth. It's better to keep your two cents!

"And the Word was made flesh, and dwelt among us, (and we beheld his glory, the glory as of the only begotten of the Father,) full of grace and truth. John bare witness of him, and cried, saying, This was he of whom I spake, He that cometh after me is preferred before me; for he was before me. And of his fulness have all we received, and grace for grace. For the law was given by Moses, but grace and truth came by Jesus Christ" (John 1:14-17).

Jesus was full of grace and if we have Him in us, *we ought also to be full of grace.* For we have all received of His fulness grace upon grace. The New Covenant is that we are not now under the law, but under grace and truth. Which way do you think God would be smarter—by making a law for us to keep, or by giving us grace? The point I want to emphasize is that we must return to a *continual, conscious placing of our faith in the grace of God for all our needs.* Whatever our problem or need, whatever our weakness or temptation, whatever our battle, the Bible says Jesus is full of grace upon grace. I believe that God will give us grace to overcome every sin. If we preach holiness without preaching grace, we'll have people in despair. Yet we must never compromise with sin on any level. God expects us to keep every one of the ten commandments. He expects us to keep every verse of Scripture in the New Testament. He expects us to love our neighbor as ourselves, and to love Him with all our heart, mind, and soul. God expects us to have no deliberate sin or willful sin in our life at all. But it's not enough to tell people, "You must be holy." The question is, "How?"— and the answer is *by faith in Jesus, by calling on God, by grace.* If we will say, "God, give me grace to overcome this sin," God will do it. Jesus is full of grace, grace upon grace. How can we change? Only by grace.

Paul constantly refers to grace, for example, "According to the *grace* that is given me." He states in 1 Corinthians 15:10, "But by the *grace* of God I am what I am. And His *grace* which was bestowed upon me was not in vain; but I labored more abundantly than they all: yet not I, but the *grace of God* which was with me." It is by the grace of God that we are pure. It is by the grace of God that we have certain gifts (Romans 12:6). It is by the grace of God that we have various callings (2 Timothy 1:9). It is grace that makes us what we are. Notice how careful Paul is to give God the credit and the glory. Every one of us, whatever progress we have made with God, is obliged to say with Paul, "By the *grace of God* I am what I am." It wasn't our works, or our spirituality, or our goodness. It was the extent to which we trusted God for grace!

It is possible to waste grace. Paul didn't waste the grace which was bestowed upon him. It was not in vain. Our free will plays a decisive role here as elsewhere in the Christian life. We must *choose* to believe and trust God for grace. Then let that grace work within us as Paul did. Look up out of the pit, become Jesus-conscious instead of sin-conscious. This is a basic principle! Continually put your faith in the grace of our Lord Jesus Christ and you will change.

Paul, speaking of his call to the ministry, states in Ephesians 3:7-8, "Whereof I was made a minister, according to *the gift of the grace* of God given unto me by the effectual working of his power. Unto me, who am less than the least of all saints, is *this grace given,* that I should preach among the Gentiles the unsearchable riches of Christ." Do you know why Paul was so mightily used of God? It is because he knew he was nothing. He had no faith in himself at all. He was totally and completely dependent upon God. The very key to Paul's life is that he really considered himself less than the least of the saints and therefore he trusted God openly and in all circumstances for grace. I know of few Christians today who consider themselves less than the least of all saints.

Take a look at your own opinion of yourself. Can you honestly say that you consider yourself less than the weakest Christian you know? Most of us know very well we're not less than the least and that's exactly what's wrong with us. If we would see how rotten we are, we would have no faith left in our works. With no faith left in our works, we would be forced to look to Jesus. And when we put our total trust in Jesus, then we'll be given grace to become more like Him.

Do you believe in the grace message? Or are you one of those who goes about establishing his own righteousness? The Pharisees were extremely religious. They never missed a church service, they fasted twice a week, they tithed everything, even down to anise and cumin, a couple of garden herbs. They went out and counted their carrots and gave every tenth carrot to the Lord. They were more religious than anyone you can imagine, but they were as lost as could be because they still trusted their works for salvation. Their faith wasn't in the Lord Jesus, their faith was entirely in themselves. Their attitude was one of pride for themselves and scorn and disdain for others. "Look at us, we faithfully obey all the commandments; the rest of you little peons aren't really walking with God. Why do your disciples pluck corn in the corn field? Why don't they wash their hands before they eat? What are you doing healing on the Sabbath, Jesus? You're breaking all of our rules!" They were religious, strictly religious, but they were sadly lost. Are there any Pharisees in the Church today? I sense too many of us may have a touch of the Pharisee in our attitudes and actions. We have to decide what and whom we're trusting. If it is religion, in any aspect, instead of Jesus, we're in trouble.

Peter states in 1 Peter 4:10, "As every man hath received the gift, even so minister the same one to another, as *good stewards of the manifold grace of God.*" If you have received any gift, then share it, minister it, use it as a means of service. The word "manifold" means "many varied" grace of God. Why does one person have a gift different from another? It's the manifold grace of God— the many gifts of grace from God. If a person has the gift of healing, did he get it because he was more spiritual? No, he received it by grace. If a person is called to preach or teach in the office of a pastor or a teacher, did he receive that calling because he was more spiritual? No! He got it because of grace. Many laymen are far more spiritual than their pastor. Jacob and Esau provide the perfect illustration of grace versus works. They were called while they were still in the womb, neither one having done anything good or bad. You don't get a call by your works, you get a call by grace.

Hebrews 4:14-17 gives us a glimpse of the unfathomable grace and mercy of our Lord.

> "Seeing then that we have a great high priest, that is passed into the heavens, Jesus the Son of God, let us hold fast our profession. For we have not an high priest which cannot be touched with the feelings of our infirmities; but was in all points tempted like as we are, yet without sin. Let us therefore come boldly unto the *throne of grace,* that we may obtain mercy, and *find grace to help in time of need."*

Anytime we have a need, no matter how large or small, we are invited to take that need directly to Jesus, our great High Priest. Not to some saint on earth, not to some preacher, but to Jesus, the very Son of God, Who has passed into the heavens. I have an "in" with God because I know the One who sits on God's right hand personally. He's a good friend of mine, He's my Savior, and His name is Jesus. Jesus, though He is God incarnate, yet knows and understands our every problem and temptation. He was tempted in every way we could ever be tempted. He was tempted to get discouraged. He was tempted to say,

"Phooey on the whole bunch of those disciples." He was tempted to fall down and worship the devil. He was tempted by prestige, pride, status. He was tempted to throw in the towel, tempted in all points like as we are, yet without sin. *It is not a sin to be tempted.* It is only a sin to say "Yes" to it, to yield to it, to give in to it. Our Lord experienced every type of temptation, yet He stood firm against Satan, as we can.

Because of our wonderful Savior, our High Priest seated on the right hand of God, we can come boldly unto the throne of grace. The name of that throne is the "throne of grace!" "You mean You won't judge me, God? I thought if I came to Your throne You would say, 'You wicked sinner, you blew it again.'" No, we can come to the *throne of grace* to obtain mercy. That applies to sin. You don't need mercy if you haven't blown it. Jesus has died, He's already paid the penalty for your sin, He has already been damned for it. Walk up to God boldly and say, "God, I don't deserve to be here, *but I see one word written on your throne, GRACE,* and here I am and I need You. Have mercy on me, help me, it's a time of need for me." Don't give up, don't adjust to your sin, come to the throne of grace in time of need. The devil will tell you that God is waiting to chastise you, but God wants to help you more than you want to be helped. *His throne is the throne of grace, not judgment, for all those who are being saved.*

The Bible says in Romans 8:26 that the Spirit helps our infirmities or weaknesses. The devil says, "You've blown it! You're so weak, you're such a lousy Christian. Give up! Throw in the towel. You'll never make it." But the Bible says *the Holy Spirit helps our weaknesses.* If we don't have any weaknesses, we don't need the Holy Spirit. If we're perfect, we don't need God; but personally, I need the Holy Spirit to help my infirmities. I still blow my cool.

I'm still impatient. At times, I find myself getting apathetic. I find myself needing a new touch from God, needing fire again. I find myself in a desperate need for a new hunger and thirst for righteousness. Where am I going to get it? In front of the throne of grace, and that's where you'll get it, too!

The Scriptures tell us to come *boldly* to the throne of grace. We think surely, if we're allowed to approach at all, we ought to crawl. But we are to come boldly, not like whipped pups, because Jesus has shed His blood and died on the cross for our sins.

Most of us still are filled with pride, wanting to take credit for any righteousness we may have. But if anybody is anything at all, it is by grace. Who gets the credit for that? Jesus Christ gets the credit. If there is someone whom God uses, it is by grace. There is no room for boasting, except in the Lord. If you have a happy marriage today, it is by grace. If you are saved today, it is by grace. If you are pure in your actions, it's by grace. If you are gentle and meek and kind, it's because of grace, not because of your own goodness.

I was saved by grace and I'm not going to switch horses. Jesus has been gracious to me. He has kept me even when I didn't want to be kept. He has kept me clean and pure and holy. He still has a lot of work to do, but I'm going to keep trusting Jesus. It is by grace that I'll be made like Him, not by my goodness or works.

So, dear reader, go humbly before the throne of grace. God "gives grace to the humble" (1 Peter 5:5). Put your faith in God's grace for deliverance, victory, and consistency. Come boldly to the throne of grace to obtain mercy and to find grace to help in time of need.

God is bound—bound by His Word; He is obligated to come through for you!

Choose to allow Him to make of you all that He desires

you to be. Choose to let Him conform you into the image of His beloved Son. By prayer, at His throne of grace, *you can change.*

Be not deceived; no matter what your circumstances are—YOU HAVE THE FREEDOM TO CHOOSE!

EPILOGUE

Choose This Day . . .

"Choose this day whom you will serve . . . but as for me and my house we will serve the Lord." (Joshua 24:15)

This epilogue is intended as a summary in which we wish to give specific help on how to experience freedom in Christ. If you've not read the rest of the book please do so, rather than try to take short cuts by skipping to this chapter. Indeed, after praying the following prayers it would be good if you went through the entire book again.

The first step to freedom is to accept for yourself the free gift of the redemptive work of Jesus Christ on the cross. If you have never welcomed Him into your heart and life, pause right now and open your heart to Him through the following prayer.

> Dear Jesus, I believe You are the Son of God. I believe all my sins, the smallest ones and the worst ones, the whole stack of my sin was nailed to You. Wash me with Your blood as clean as You are. I believe You died for my sin and bore my guilt and my judgment. I accept You as my Savior, and I call on You as Lord, to be my Lord. Take over my life. Come inside of me and live Your life through me. Through Your name, Jesus, I pray.

Now, at all cost to your pride, *you must forgive* every single person who has hurt you, wounded you, betrayed your confidence, let you down, faked their love, etc. You must not allow resentment, jealousy, bitterness, or hate to remain in you. Hate is an open door for Satanic oppression and control. If you've not already done so, ask the Holy Spirit to drop into your mind every person you need to forgive. Ask Jesus' blood to cleanse the resentment and hurts out. If you need additional help in this area, review chapter one and read Matthew 6:12-15; Ephesians 4:30-32; Colossians 3:13-15; as well as Matthew 18:21-35.

If you have in the past at any time been *involved in the occult,* whether seriously or just from the motive of curiosity, it must be renounced. The occult has many forms: drugs, ouija board, palmistry, fortunetelling, astral projection, horoscopes, ESP, mental telepathy, witchcraft, Satan-worship, Eastern religions, hypnosis, etc. You must confess these involvements as sin, specifically renounce them and repent of them and command the spirits to loose you and let you go as in the prayer below.

One spirit that has not been stressed, but which is very common, even among Christians, is a *spirit of heaviness* (Isaiah 61:3). It is one of the most unnoticed Satanic oppressions. Many Christians suffer from severe depression. The enemy gets away with this spirit; it is easily overlooked and few realize the danger of a spirit of heaviness. Renounce and repent of this spirit and command it to go as in the prayer below.

Another area in which we must guard ourselves is *worry, fretting, and anxiety.* Worry is the opposite of believing in prayer. 1 Peter 5:7 tells us to cast all our care upon Him, for He cares for us. This verse is absolutely worthless unless you do it. Ask the Holy Spirit to drop into your mind every single thing that you're worried or burdened over. Most people receive between ten and forty situations, families, or problems. It is absolutely amazing.

You must then, one by one, specifically cast these things onto Jesus.

Another area of concern is guilt. If you do not really believe that you're forgiven, you should read the following verses of Scripture and then pray and believe them. Psalm 103:8-14; Isaiah 55:7-9; Hosea 14:4; Micah 7:18-19; Romans 5:1; Hebrews 10:17; 1 John 1:9. Stand on the Word of God, not what you feel. If your faith is in your feelings, your faith is in you, because your feelings are part of you.

Also, we must make sure that we have total victory in the area of *unclean spirits*. We must make sure that we are free of lust, fornication, seduction, hating men or women, masturbation, perversion, etc. These things must be specifically renounced and turned from, instead of justified.

The last area is of vital concern. It is the spirit of rebellion. Rebellion is the very nature of Satan himself. To be a Christian means to be a member of the Kingdom of God, or under the government of God. A kingdom is the domain of a king. To be in the Kingdom of God means you are under the domain or dominion of Jesus. Jesus, the King, rules and reigns over you. The New Testament is no longer a "guide" for your life that offers nice "tidbits" of information; the New Testament is the commandment of King Jesus. It is not optional, whether you obey it or not. You simply salute Jesus, say "Yes Sir!" and do what He bids. Only as we come under the authority of the King— Jesus—are we really in the Kingdom of God. All demon control traces back to rebellion to God's authority over our lives. All sin is lawlessness (1 John 3:4). Until we really accept Jesus as our King and His Word as the authority of God over us, we will never be free. The truth shall set you free. We must renounce all rebellion and the spirit of rebellion. To repent of rebellion is to renounce the attitude and nature of Satan and to accept the rule of God's government.

These are the seven catagories that I believe are root causes for physical or mental sickness: *unforgiveness* (resentment), *the occult, a spirit of heaviness* (depression), *worry, guilt, uncleanness,* and *rebellion.* Now make the following command for each of these seven areas. Deliverance is not a prayer to God, but rather a command to Satan in the name of God, that is, in Jesus' name. Passivity is a dangerous stance spiritually. When we are under satanic attack, we must rise up with all our will and resistance and command Satan to flee.

> I renounce you, Satan, and all your principalities, powers, rulers, and spirits and all your evil work. I sever all relationships with you. I choose the will of God and reject your will. I take back all ground given to you. I repent and renounce all evil spirits, especially _____. I renounce their control and authority over me. Satan, you will not have dominion over me! I take dominion and authority over you in the name of Jesus Christ: I command you to loose me and to let me go.

Now believe in Bible faith that it is done, because of Who Jesus is, and the authority that is in His name. "Whosoever shall call on the name of the Lord shall be delivered" (Joel 2:32). God said it; I believe it; that settles it!

We must reiterate the fact that in maintaining our deliverance we must understand the principle of controlling our thoughts. Review that chapter. We must understand how to judge our own thoughts. Thoughts come from three sources: our senses, the Holy Spirit, or evil spirits. Any thought that does not agree with Scripture we must not accept. *Just because a thought comes into our mind, does not mean that it's true.*

Consistent attendance at anointed church services,

regular personal devotions, and daily praying in the Spirit (tongues) will assist in staying strong spiritually and therefore being able to resist the enemy. We have found that no one makes any progress without these three aspects of the Christian life. It's important to cease being a wanderer from church to church. I encourage you to submit yourself to some Spirit-filled elders who can guide you. Allow your roots to grow instead of wandering from church to church and being a "blessing-seeker." If you transplant a tree every two or three weeks around your yard, it will die. I sincerely believe that you will hinder your growth in Christ unless you get in one church under sound spiritual authority and stay there. We have found this true in our local church. Those who have stayed in our church have had their needs met. The wanderers never obtain liberty from their sins or demonic oppression.

Also, the matter of regular personal devotions could hardly be overstressed. The Lord wants us to have a personal "Presence" every single morning. The reason I use the word *presence* is that you can read the Bible or pray without the Presence of God. Obviously, that kind of devotional life is valueless. You should get into the Presence of the Lord at the beginning of every day. As you go through the day, neglect not the gift that is in you, but pray in tongues constantly. Whenever Satan tries to attack you with attitudes, irritableness, or evil thoughts, simply begin praying silently to yourself in the Spirit or in tongues. Few Spirit-filled Christians understand the value of speaking in tongues. Tongues is far more than the evidence of the baptism in the Holy Spirit. Praying in tongues is the supernatural prayer means of staying full of the Holy Spirit, hour by hour and day by day!

Finally, this is my prayer for all of you, who by the providence of God, have read this book:

"Now may the God of peace, that brought again from the dead our Lord Jesus. that great shepherd of the sheep, through the blood of the everlasting covenant, Make you perfect in every good work to do his will, working in you that which is well-pleasing in his sight, through Jesus Christ; to whom be glory for ever and ever. Amen." (Hebrews 13:20-21)

APPENDIX

List of Scriptures against spiritualism, witchcraft, sorcery, etc.

OLD TESTAMENT	NEW TESTAMENT
Exodus 7:11-12	Acts 7:39-43
(2 Tim. 3:8)	(Amos 5:26-27)
22:18	8:5-25
	16:16-18
Leviticus 19:26, 31	19:13-20
20:6-8, 27	
	1 Corinthians 10:20-22
Deuteronomy 4:19	
7:25-26	2 Corinthians 11:13-15
13:1-18	
17:2-7	Galatians 5:19-21
18:9-22	
26:14	2 Timothy 3:8
1 Samuel 15:22-23	Revelation 18:23
28:3-25 (see	21:8
next reference)	22:15
1 Chronicles 10:13-14	
2 Kings 17:17-18	
21:5-6	
23:24	
Isaiah 2:6	
8:19-22	
47:12-15, 8:11	
45:22	
Jeremiah 8:1-3	
10:2	
27:9-10	
Ezekiel 13:1-23	
21:21	
Hosea 4:12	
Micah 5:12	
Zechariah 10:1-2	
Malachi 3:5	

ABOUT THE AUTHOR

Ernest J. Gruen is the son of a devout American Baptist deacon. He was converted at the age of nine and called to preach ten years later. Both of these experiences occurred in American Baptist churches. He served as an American Baptist pastor for ten years. He received his B.A. degree from Friends University (Wichita, Kansas) where he graduated with honors, and his B.D. degree from Central Baptist Theological Seminary in Kansas City, Kansas.

Currently, he is the pastor of the Full Faith Church of Love in Kansas City, Kansas. The Full Faith Church of Love is a Spirit-filled church made up of people of all denominations. The church transcends all sociological barriers. It is an unusual church, in that it has no membership and has never taken up an offering. An offering box is at the back of the church for anyone who wishes to contribute. Also, the church believes in the plurality of elders. The elders make all decisions by unanimous agreement. They operate under the principle that the local church is a theocracy. All the elders pray until they're in unanimous agreement on how Jesus Himself would vote. They believe the only vote that counts is Jesus' vote and they pray until they have His mind, together. The Full Faith Church of Love became a "Jesus people" center with a congregation that is 50 percent young people. The church grew from an attendance of 150 to 1,200 in a four year period, making it one of the fastest growing churches in the Kansas City area.

On Christmas night of 1965, Pastor Gruen knew there had to be "something more to Christianity" than what he'd experienced. After praying for five hours he had a definite second experience of crucifixion and resurrection life. Five months later he was baptized in the Holy Spirit. He has done extensive ministry among Catholics and many Protestant denominations. He also speaks at various college campuses throughout the midwest.